more of **Nenagh's Yesterdays**

199 Photographs • 2,000 Faces • 1890s to 1980s

Front Cover: see page 27.

Page 1: **'The Bleeding Horse'** was a knight of the road named Kelly. His family owned the Bleeding Horse public house in Camden St, Dublin. Mr Kelly stayed in lodging houses during his two or three week sojourn in Nenagh. One such lodgings was 'The Mansion', the two-storey house in the right-hand row of John's Lane, seen in photograph No. 41 of *Nenagh Yesterday*. A fellow-patron betimes was Johnny Deegan, of the same vocation, variously known as 'Smiler', 'Johnny Forty Coats', and 'Belsie Bow'.

Mr Kelly was self-sufficient financially, being in receipt of a pension for service with the British Army in India. He was captured in this hail or farewell pose by Jack Ryan (probably in the 1930s) at the entrance to Anderson's Well on the New Line/Well Rd, re-erected nearby in the early 1980s by the ESB outside their offices.

Page 128: (*top of this page*) **The Kennedy Concert.** Harriett and Nellie Kennedy conducted classes in etiquette, dancing and singing, at No. 14 Summerhill. Their pupils gave an annual concert in the Institute hall.
Back (l to r): Gloria O'Boyle, Carmel O'Boyle, Annette O'Boyle. **Front:** Michael Ryan, Mary O'Driscoll, Finn O'Driscoll.

Back Cover: (*middle of this page*) **'The White Knight',** was the name by which this ice-cream vending machine was known around town, at hurling matches, and at sunny Dromineer. (l to r): John O'Dwyer, owner, 79 Pearse St; Joseph McDonnell, salesman, better known as Jonie Hickey; Dick Bourke, 81-2 Pearse St; Miss Spain.

Rory Hope you haven't this already

Enagh.

more of **Nenagh's Yesterdays**

Compiled by
Nancy Murphy
& Fiona O'Brien

Editorial:
Elaine Burke Houlihan
& Donal A. Murphy

Published by

Published in 1997 by
RELAY BOOKS
Tyone, Nenagh, Co. Tipperary
(067) 31734

*The book is published
with the support of Tipperary Leader Group*

ISBN 0 946327 23 8

British Library Cataloguing-in-Publication Data
A catalogue record for this book
is available from the British Library

Design and typesetting: in-house by RELAY

Typeface: Times, 11 pt on auto
Page size: 248 x 186 mm

Printed by Nenagh Guardian Ltd. on 100gr art

Dear Waldron, permit me to tell you
    I'm landed in Nenagh at last,
The place seems remarkably tidy–
    The women are stylish and and fast.
The Dead bell is constantly ringing
    In Nenagh each day since I came,
Some say that the water's corrupted
    And others that whiskey's to blame.

I paid the Miss Tuohys a visit,
    And slipped off my beat on the sly,
To take a few mugs of mulled porter
    For I was most horribly dry…
We've Gubbins, and Buggles and Acres,
    A Spain, and a Hough, and a Clear,
We've Minogues, and Whiteheads, and Austins,
    All bungled together up here.

We've Clampets, Corneilles, and Toohers,
    A Day, and a Coyne, and a Pine,
And all the strange names you could mention,
    Expecting this old one of mine.
We've Cunneens, and Tumpanes, and Cadells,
    A Woodhouse, as well as a Poe,
McCommiskeys, Muggivans, Chumneys,
    And others that yet I don't know.

– as Sergeant Jack Keily saw us upon his arrival in 1887.

Contents

Acknowledgements

We included photographs and biographies in *Nenagh Yesterday* (pp. 11-13) of Nenagh's principal photographers up to the 1980s – Kevin O'C Bernal, Samuel Bernal, William J Heaney and Jack Ryan. The number of pages governs the amount of photographs and so this book has given us an opportunity to print some more of their work that did not fit into *Nenagh Yesterday*.

We have made every effort to trace the authorship of photographs accurately; if there are any errors we will be glad to correct them in a future volume. It may also have happened, because of the extent of identification of subjects, that errors in that respect have slipped through; in any such cases also we will welcome corrections and publish them.

Anon: 2, 10, 20, 25, 40, 55, 56, 57, 65, 69, 81, 97, 109, 111, 112, 121, 123, 126, 129, 145, 150, 153, 154, 157, 158, 159, 162,181, 183, 184, 191, 192, page 128, Back cover; **Kevin O'C Bernal:** 34, 35, 36, 37, 38, 42, 44, 115, 116, 141, 147, 148, 149, 152, 160, 161, 164, 182; **Samuel Bernal:** 193; **Anne Brennan:** 27, 165, 166; **Martin J. Carroll Studio:** 139; **Paddy Cotter,** *Midland Tribune*: 163; **Kathleen Duggan:** 138; **Eason Collection, NLI:** 17, 24; **Paul Flynn:** 155; **John D. Gleeson:** 43; **P. Gleeson:** 131; **William J Heaney:** 19, 66, 117, 120, 124, 130, 143, 144, 194; *Irish Times*: 64; **Lafayette, Dublin:** 142; **Lawrence Collection, NLI:** 1, 3, 11, 22, 32, 41, 48, 49, 50; **Lawrence Collection (new series):** 8, 21; **John Long,** *The Guardian*: 99, 100, 103, 125, 178, 179, 185, 195, 196; **Tommy Lynch:** 128; **Donal A Murphy:** 4, 5, 6, 9, 12, 14, 18, 26, 52, 53, 54, 58, 59, 60, 61, 62, 63, 67, 68, 74, 75, 76, 77, 78, 79, 82, 93, 94, 95, 98, 102, 104, 105, 106, 108,122, 127, 146, 156, 167, 168, 169,170, 171, 172, 173,174, 175, 176,177, 180, 186, 187, 188, 189, 190; **Nancy Murphy:** front cover, 15, 16, 23, 28, 29, 30, 31, 45, 46, 47, 51, 70, 71, 72, 88, 89, 90, 91, 92, 96; **Patrick O'Brien:** 118, 119; **Oliver O'Gorman:** 7, 13; **John O'Grady:** 101; **Jack Ryan:** page 1, 33, 39, 73, 80, 83, 84, 85, 86, 87, 107, 132, 133, 134, 135, 136, 137, 140; **John Shoer:** 151.

Listed hereafter in alphabetical order are the names of those, in addition to the above, who have contributed in any way in the compilation of this book, i.e. advice, identification, loaning of photographs, etc.

Anne Barry, Toni Brophy, Mick Burns, Denis Butler, Paddy Cadell, Nancy Carey, Dr Maureen Carmody, Noel Cleary, Noel & Maureen Clifford, Mary Coonan, Micheál Corrigan, Joe Daly, Una Darcy, Sinéad Devaney, Larry Dunne, Dessie Finn, Seán Finn, Denis Finnerty, Sally Gardiner, Tony Geaney, Michael & Grace Gilmartin, Johnny Gleeson, Seamus Gleeson, Richie Grace, Sr Patricia Greene, Anthony Hanly, Jimmy Hayes, Nellie Herriott, David Hodgins, Mary Hogan, Sid Houlihan, Michael Hynes, Pat Hynes, Sr Assumpta Kearns, Garda Billy Kelly & colleagues, John Kennedy, Fiona Lewis, Frank Lewis, Ger Lewis, P. J. Maxwell, Marguerite McGrath, Johnny McGrath, Jim Meagher & Castle Brand staff, Michael Moloney, Teddy Morgan, Donal Morrissey, Billy Murphy, John & Phil Nagle, Donie Nealon, Anne O'Brien, Denis O'Brien, Michael O'Brien, Kathleen O'Dwyer, Lisa O'Gorman, Noel O'Meara, Gerry O'Rourke, Seamus O'Shea, Alice Ryan, Michael Ryan, Patrick A. Ryan, Dessie & Noreen Ryan & family, John Scroope, Phyllis Shoer, Brendan Treacy, Peggy Tynan, Paschal Whelan.

Can Timmy Save Toyland? by Vincent McDonnell

Toyland is disappearing. A hole in the ozone layer is causing the ice to melt. Timmy appeals to grown-ups for help when he appears on the Latest Latest Show. Mister Carbuncle and his henchmen have a ghastly plan to speed up the disaster. And they hold Katie, Timmy's little sister, hostage so that no-one dare stop them. It involves ingenuity and daring to hitch a lift to the North Pole in the villain's giant aerosol cans. There are setbacks and exciting developments … If you like a funny, clever and action-packed read this book should entertain you. Suitable for young readers up to 13 years. – *Irish Farmers Journal*, Feb 1996. *18 line drawings & perforated flap for tear-off Bookmark.*
144 pp., IR£3.95/$7.95, pb, 0946327 22 X

A trip through Tipperary Lakeside by Nancy Murphy

By the River Shannon's Lough Derg scenic routes: the attractions and amenities, environment, and historical snippets, through the eyes of a hiker, cyclist, or driver on the Portumna-Nenagh-Ballina roads and side roads to the lake villages of Lough Derg on the river Shannon. *26 colour and 14 black and white photographs, 2 maps, 1 line drawing.*
96 pp., IR£3.95/$7.95, pb, 0946327 21 1

Literature in Ireland: Studies Irish and Anglo-Irish by Thomas MacDonagh

Reprint of the 1916 classic. With an introduction by Gerald Dawe, poet, critic, and lecturer. What is truly amazing is how little this work has dated. … Nancy Murphy's biographical profile is a model of its kind: succinct but comprehensive, analytic but also winning in its humanising evocation of the man, his family, his contemporaries, his society. – *The Nationalist*, May 1996. The things that attracted him to me, as revealed in this book, were his powers of analysis, his love for and promotion of the Irish language, and his quality as an educator. – *Luke Murtagh, CEO of Tipperary (NR) VEC, launching the book.*
xvi + 209 pp., IR£7.95/$15.95, pb, 0 946327 16 5

Portrait of a Parish: Monsea and Killodiernan, Co. Tipperary by Daniel Grace

A truly magnificent, thorough and well-organised account by the founder president of the Ormond Historical Society of North Tipperary area from earliest recorded times to the present day – its land, antiquities, and people and their lives, and events, institutions, buildings, industries, sports, names, and heaven knows what not, with sources cited and the whole indexed by name and place. Upmarket, academic, good value. – *Books Ireland*, Nov 1996.
xii + 346 pp., 130 photographs, 17 maps & ills, IR£12.00/$24.00, pb, 0 946327 17 3

Tipperary: A Treasure Chest Compiled by Elaine Burke Houlihan

It's a book that plucks at the heart strings, entertains, stirs the memory of other days. – *The Guardian*, Jan 1996. In several respects this is one of the most attractive books to come out out of the county for some years. Visually and technically … it is a delight to the eye. … astonishing value at the price.– *Tipperary Historical Journal,* 1995. History and hurling, marriage and murder, politics and piseogs, romance and roguery. As with any treasure chest, we could keep picking and choosing from this well nigh inexhaustible hoard. – *The Tipperary Star*, Dec 1995.
204 pp., IR£6.95/$13.95, pb, 0946327 15 7

The Two Tipperarys
by Donal A. Murphy

By any standards this is a *tour de force* … the style of writing is colourful, arresting and at times witty. It is scholarship at its best and the results of many years research in the author's own county. – *Administration, Spring 1995* … traces in masterly fashion the campaign for dividing the county with all its complexities, intrigues and surprises. … a delight for the serious student of political lobbying, local government and administrative evolution. … The copious notes, conveniently placed at the end of each chapter, offer many illuminating and entertaining profiles of the colourful characters. – *Limerick Leader*, Feb 1995.
xxvi + 342 pp., IR£9.95/$19.90 [reduced price], pb, 0 946327 14 9

Walkabout Nenagh
by Nancy Murphy

A racy profile of its streets, buildings and personalities.
… is principally about people: those who achieved national or international fame, those who played a significant role in the commercial, political or cultural life of the town. – *The Guardian*, Dec 1994.
139 pp., 12 photographs (including a 1933 aerial of Nenagh), 14 line drawings, a centre-page map of the town.
IR£5.00/$10.00 [reduced price], pb, 0 946327 12 2

Nenagh Castle – chronology and architecture
Compiled by Nancy Murphy

A concise survey of the history of the first Butler headquarters through the travail of centuries – the Norman-Gaelic-English encounters in microcosm.
8 pp., IR£1.00/$2.00, pb, 0946327 10 6

Nenagh Yesterday
Compiled by Brendan Treacy

199 photographs, 1890s-1970s, each with extensive captions. Ireland in miniature: one town in nostalgic depth. A valuable social history, teeming with pictures of milestone occasions and the people who made them.
Nenagh Yesterday … a gem of a book. … marvellous collection, embellished by Nancy Murphy's historical and biographical script … – *The Guardian*, Dec 1993.
144 pp., IR£10.00/$20.00, pb, 0946327 11 4

Forthcoming Titles

The Last Lords of Ormond: The Cromwellian Plantation in the 'Countrie of the Three O'Kennedys', Dermot F. Gleeson (1938, updated 1997). An outstanding regional study which spans the Tyrone rebellion, an abortive plantation of 1625-39 under Strafford, through the war of 1641-52 and plantation, to the Restoration settlement, the Williamite war and the '1688 Forfeitures'. Updated by an introduction by Daniel Grace, and a 17th c. chronology placing the events in Ormond in the context of Irish and English-Scottish developments.

The Cormack Brothers: Their Trial, Execution and Exhumation, Nancy Murphy. The 1858 execution and 1910 exhumation have made a deep imprint in Tipperary lore. A classic case of a miscarriage of justice?

RELAY's books are available from good bookshops/newsagents in Ireland, and the following:
Relay Books, Tyone, NENAGH, Co. Tipperary, Ireland, Tel: (067) 31734, Fax: (067) 33586
Robert Towers, 2 The Crescent, Monkstown, CO. DUBLIN, Ireland. Tel: (01) 2806532, Fax: (01) 2806020
Irish Books and Media, The Franklin Business Center, 1433 Franklin Ave East, MINNEAPOLIS, MN55404-2135, USA, Tel: (612) 871-3505, Fax: (612) 871-3358

Please add IR£2.00/$3.50 [delivery by Surface Mail] for 1 book and IR£0.50/$1.00 for each additional book.

Nenagh Yesterday – Amendments

No. 29: Bulfin Crescent was built in a field behind the Birr Road houses and the residents were allocated new houses in the same sequence. The old terrace was then demolished.

No. 41: John's Lane, photographed in the 1970s, not the l940s when all the houses were still occupied. The final paragraph was written for a different picture which looked towards the CBS. The houses on the left: 'Gag' Maher who reared champion boxers – Jackie, Patsy and Micksie; Costelloe, McMahon, Butler, – , Maher, Gunnell, O'Meara the cobbler, Delahunty the tailor; on the right: Moroney, 'Mary from Nenagh' who made Peggy's Leg sweets, 'Moll the Daw', Cleary/McLoughlin, Cleary, The Mansion (a lodging house – see page 2 – whose most regular resident was 'Assy' Kenna, the last of Nenagh's gas lamp lighters; schoolboy lore declared that the house was 'that tall' [two-storey] because 'Assy' was a very tall man), Costelloe, McCullough the barber.

No. 43, Summerhill: There is only a slice of Mattie Osborne's house in the picture. The house fully visible was owned by Margaret Mary Fitzgerald (née O'Halloran, of the monumental sculptor family), widow of Harry Fitzgerald, an ex-recruiting Sergeant in World War I who appears as a bandsman in the picture facing page 72 of E. H. Sheehan's *Nenagh and Its Neighbourhood*. Hers was next to Toohey's coalyard, itself next to the church railings. In the other direction and in a previous generation, next to Osbornes was O'Briens, then a bicycle shop, then O'Donoghues on the corner of Falvey's Lane (information from Charles Fitzgerald, New Jersey, son of Harry & M. M.).

No. 52: The above Harry Fitzgerald trained the Irish Volunteers locally.

No. 53, Nenagh UDC: While it is correct that John Ryan was first elected in 1960, he had served four years by then, having been co-opted upon the death of Paddy Ayres in January or February 1956.

No. 66, Nenagh CBS PPU: Jackie Whelan, Summerhill, is in the background.

No. 79, the pantomime: was not a Choral Society production, but one of four got under way by Christy Lally. The person behind the disguise of the big, bad wolf is actually Joe Gleeson, Benedine.

No. 91, 'Keeping an Eye on Europe': The principal figures: Chamberlain (left, with hat), J O'Rourke, St. Patrick's Tce.; Hitler, Pat Joe Ryan, Summerhill; Mussolini, Christy Finn, St. Joseph's Park.

No. 97, Draughts Club: Bill Spain's address should have been given as Gortadalaun, Ardcroney.

No. 104, County Council Golf Outing: Tom Reynolds is at the extreme right in the middle row. Tom and Kevin were sons of Joe Reynolds who resided at the Courthouse in the section later occupied by the Committee of Agriculture offices.

No. 107, Éire Óg 1957: The man in the back row between Seán Duignan and Pat Stack is probably Buddy Tuohy, Turnpike/Ormond Street.

No. 116, Nenagh Olympic: Noel Quirke, Silvermines, is the person unidentified in the back row.

No. 141: Aluminium Company staff: Brian Toohey, at extreme right of the third row, was not from the Turnpike, but from Pound/Sarsfield St. He did not return to the factory but joined the Royal Navy.

No. 144, Jack Lynch's visit: Over Tommy ('Digger') Stanley's shoulder are, left, Frankie Ryan, Toomevara, and, right, Billy Meagher, Knockanpierce.

No. 146: Behind Teddy Morgan are Billy Morrissey, Knockanpierce, and James ('Buddy') Fitzpatrick, St. Patrick's Tce.

No. 179: The Thomas John Riggs-Miller (junior, born 1883) in the picture is the son of Margaret J. Bernal and Thomas John (senior, died 1895). Thomas John senior (son of Malachi Ryan) assumed the name Riggs-Miller in 1889. Thomas John junior (b. 1883) appears in the County Club picture No. 96 and was the father of John Riggs-Miller who is seen helping to cut the Nenagh Players cake in No 83.

No. 185, Carnival committee: May Cooney should have been identified as (later) Meagher, Monsea.

Acknowledgements: The photographer's full name was Michael Delahunt, Barrack St – but we don't know where his premises was in that street.

Preface

The widespread popularity of *Nenagh Yesterday*, compiled by Brendan Treacy and published in 1993, has been the main incentive in compiling *More of Nenagh's Yesterdays*.

This time the photographs have been drawn from RELAY's collection of photographs and transparencies – old and not so old; the National Library of Ireland collections; the aerials of Nenagh in Aerofilms library, England; and Brendan Treacy's ever-growing collection. Most of the Jack Ryan prints reproduced in the book were made in 1992 for Nenagh District Heritage Centre by the Lafayette Studio, Dublin, from glass plates in the Nenagh Guardian's safekeeping. The files of *The Guardian,* through the good offices of Pat Ryan and Mrs Bridget Nolan, joint Managing Directors, have been drawn on extensively for photographs and information. We are grateful to all the above for their generous co-operation. Some snapshots and some prints made from transparencies, of lesser quality, have been included because they are the only records of those persons or events.

Like *Nenagh Yesterday* this compilation is a cross-section of people, places and events from the 1890s to the early 1980s. Coincidentally, there are again 199 photographs. Where the subject of a photograph is also in *Nenagh Yesterday*, a cross-reference is inserted thus: [NY No. of photograph in *Nenagh Yesterday*].

Many of the pictures will serve to recall major developments in the town, like its first sewage treatment scheme, the opening of the new hospital and the indoor athletic stadium, and the personalities fronting them. The initiative of St. Joseph's Park residents, who brought to fruition their plan for a children's playground in 1974, deserve to be placed on permanent record. So too do the individual and team achievements of Nenagh Olympic Athletic Club in this, the club's fortieth year.

Other achievers are celebrated also in these pages: the founders of the Chamber of Commerce, Lions Club and Pitch-and-Putt club, and a set of natives and citizens who have contributed much to the life of Nenagh and Ireland, all of whom get portraits and profiles in words.

Older residents will view with nostalgia the gathering of boys on the Dublin road corner with not a motor-car, never mind a juggernaut, in sight. Social history is here in the streetscapes and shop fronts, featuring such bygone personalities as Bill Cavanagh, Dot Ewing, Dick Gough, Will Hogan, Josephine Powell, Joe Starr, Jimmy McCarthy and Christy Sherlock – all taking care of their trade. There are nurses, councillors and clerks galore; stirring chapters in the stories of Nenagh Ormond and Éire Óg are recalled; as always, many will derive the most pleasure from recognising 'Family & Friends' and schoolmates.

The cover picture is a scoop and doubly of interest, given the recently-announced plans for accessing Nenagh Castle from Pearse St.

The computer has made compilation of a book like this considerably easier. But the chore of searching out background information, names, and dates of events, is still a major one. Numerous people helped in this task and their assistance is greatly appreciated. We are also very grateful to the people who loaned very precious original photographs. Nancy Murphy's own *Walkabout Nenagh* proved invaluable in the compilation of captions.

Like *Nenagh Yesterday* this volume is an all-Nenagh production with the printing taken care of by Nenagh Guardian Ltd.

– **The RELAY Team**.

1 (*left*) **Barrack/Kenyon St.** The main focus of activity seems to be in the vicinity of Thomas Boland & Son, at No. 2, who sold produce from their Ballinaclough corn mill, and from their bakery located here. No overhead wires to interfere with the view of distant Knockadhageen, one of the Templederry line of hills. The name means 'hill of the two dykes'; remains of a hill fort still survive on the summit.

2 (*below*) **Tooher and Crowe.** Norah Tooher, with son Daniel and daughter Mary, had their bar, grocery and confectionery at No. 70 in 1901 and later. They were followed by Jerry Murphy with a bar and grocery. It became all grocery when it opened as M. J. O'Connor in 1952.

No. 69 had a double life, housing the Commercial Club on the first floor with its entrance through the private hall door.

The club flourished 1891-5, then closed and re-opened in 1906 as the Ormond Club, lasting until the 1930s. Sarah White, grocer and vintner, occupied the rest of the building. She married John Burke in 1896 and their daughter, Nora Mary, married Pat Crowe, Templederry. In time all of No. 69 was absorbed into Joseph O'Connor's expanding supermarket. [NY 33] However, 1994 saw No. 69 resume its separate identity as Finnerty's pharmacy.

3 (*above*) **Barrack St.** This long view of the full street is later than pic 1 as some extra poles have appeared, and the tree by the Bank of Ireland (now the MWHB offices) has grown taller.The postman is heading for Michael Ryan's public house at No. 64 (now O'Connor's newagency) [NY 35]. Beside the RIC barracks is the public house of Michael Hogan and his wife, Fanny (née Whealey) (1901). Nolan's private house (now An Siopa Leabhar) is between the two licensed premises. The barracks (below, left) looks the same as it did prior to its conversion into Kenyon St Market in mid-1991.

Over on the right is Carroll's Railway Hotel (now The Sportsman's Dream). Meantime it was McKenna's bar and grocery, followed by Séamus Sheahan's supermarket.

4 (*left*) **The Barracks.** This mid-eighteenth century town house, with steps and railings, was occupied by Morgan O'Meara in 1824. However, for most of its life it housed the forces of law – Resident Magistrates (RMs) in the last century, then the Royal Irish Constabulary (RIC) and their successors as of 1922, the Civic Guard/Garda Síochána, until 1986. Sergeant Jack Keily wrote to his friend Sergeant Thomas Waldron in 1887:

From base to the top of this dwelling 'Tis ten and a hundred long strides, And when I've to go to the garret I've always a pain in my sides. … Our bedroom is also an office, A thing very few would desire, We use it for eating and reading, And sleep at each side of the fire.

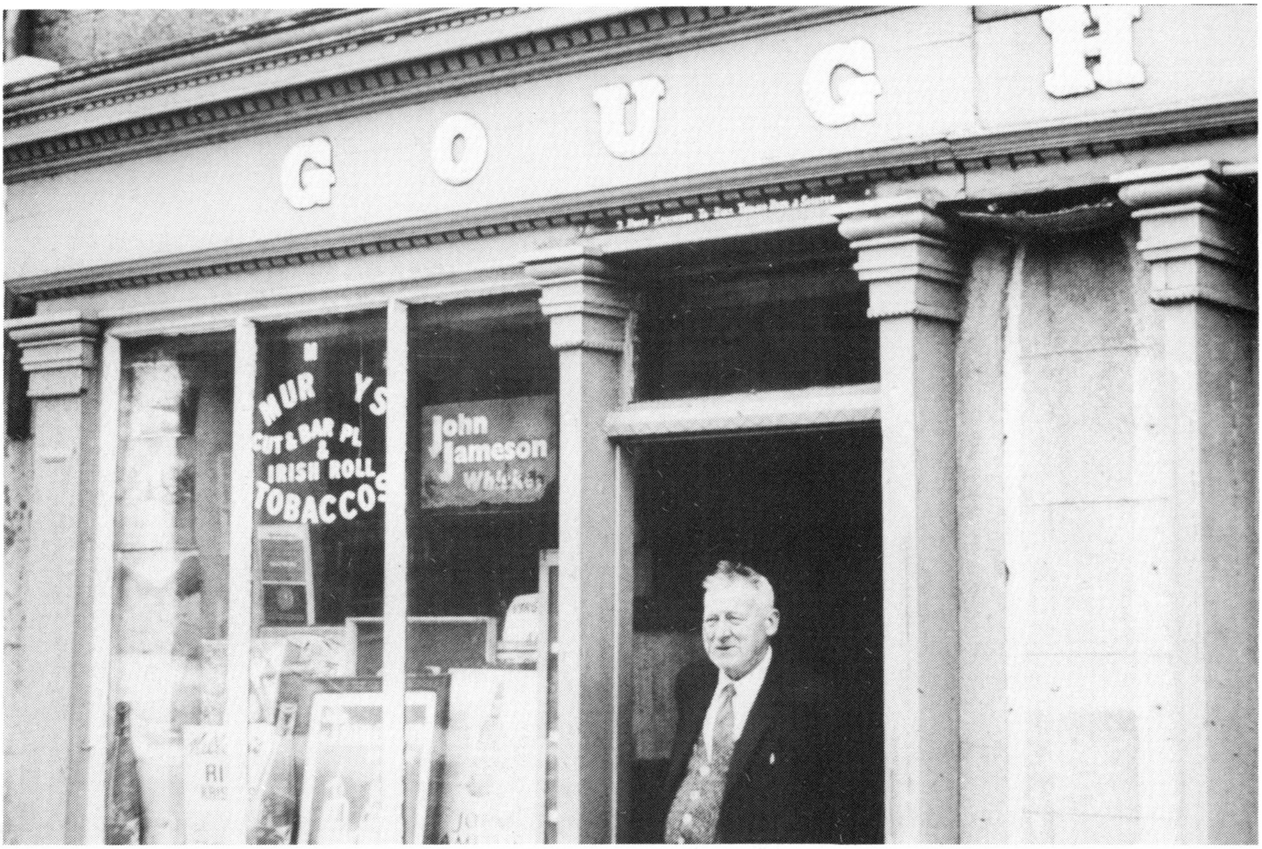
G O U G H
IRISH ROLL
TOBACCOS
John Jameson

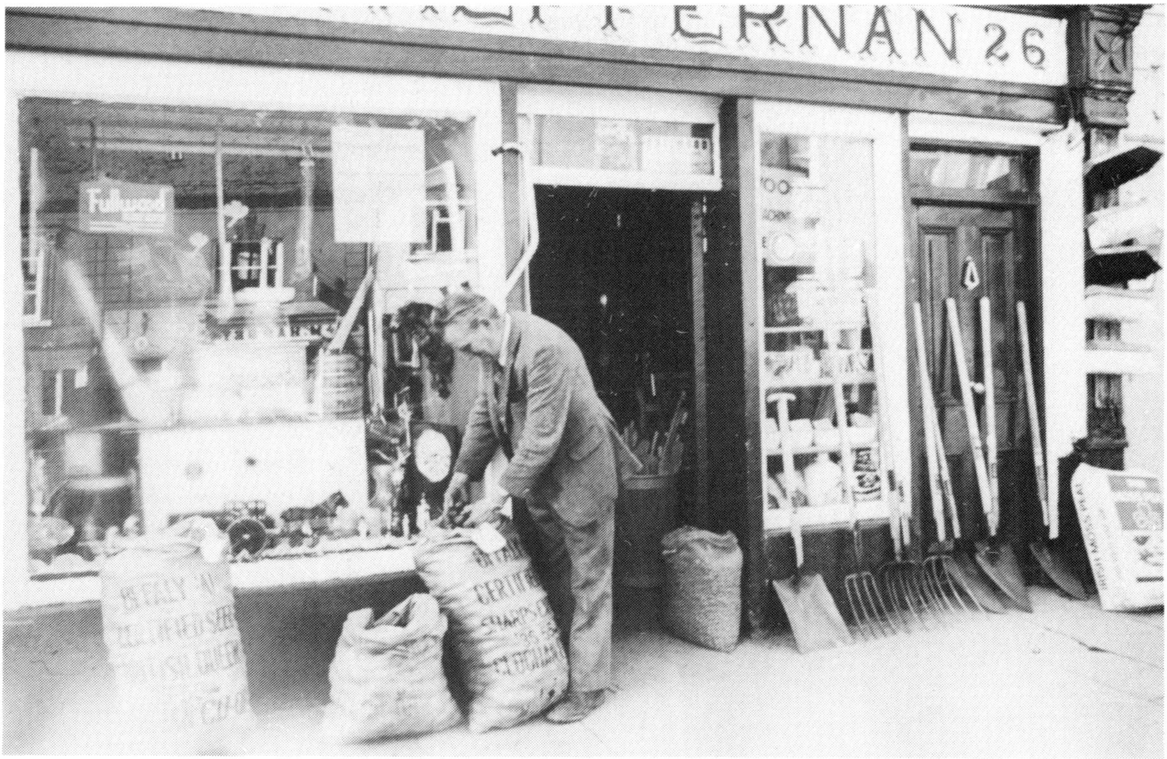
ERNAN 26

Three of Barrack/Kenyon Street's traditional shop fronts which were all replaced in recent years.

5 (*opposite, above*) Dick Gough at the door of his public house which he took over from his father, Maurice. The premises is now the offices of John Lee, auctioneer. The Gough ceramic lettering nameplate is preserved over the recreated shop in the Heritage Centre.

6 (*opposite, below*) Mick Heffernan outside his shop in No. 26. He started in Murray's hardware in Mitchel St and progresssed to opening his own business. A previous occupier was William R. Armitage (1901). The whole building was demolished in 1995 as part of the urban renewal scheme.

7 (*below*) This fine establishment with spacious yard was run by John Lee, grocer, in 1915. Later it traded as Fleming & Lee for a long period with two successive Peter Flemings at the helm. Sold out of Fleming ownership, it was refurbished as a lounge bar (now MacMathúna).

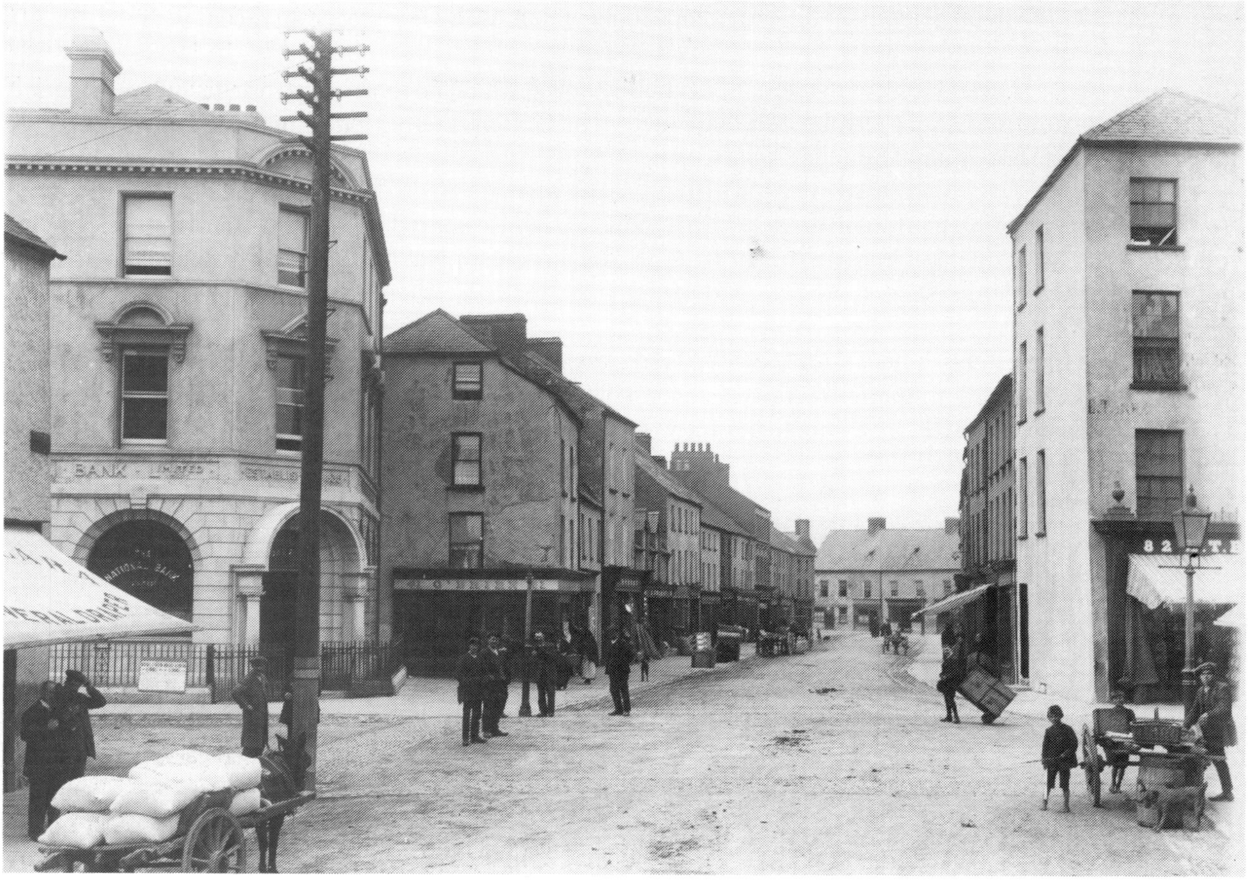
BANK LIMITED
NATIONAL BANK

PLAYER'S
Nº6
guaranteed quality
MAJOR
Gold Bond
Gold Bond
PLAYER'S
Nº6
MAJOR

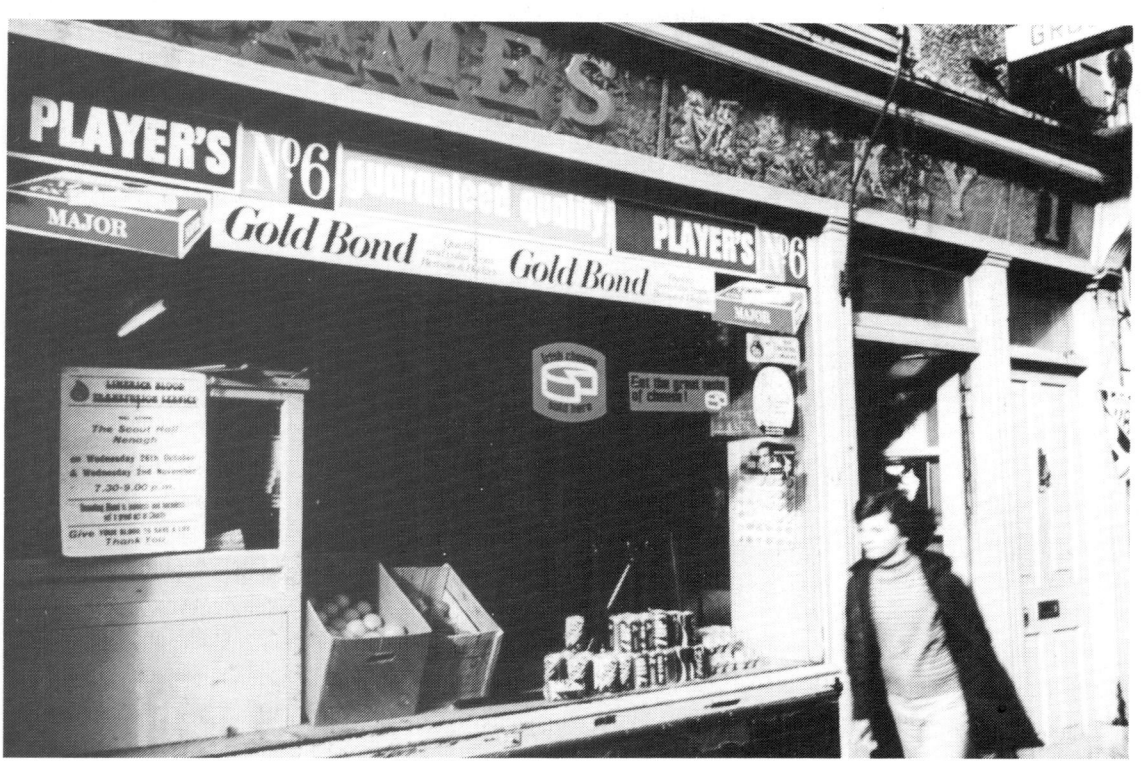

8 (*opposite, above*) The photographer said 'watch the birdie' and all movement froze at the National Bank corner. The date is circa 1915 as E. T. Bourke has replaced Corbett at No. 82 Castle/Pearse St (now Irish Nationwide) [NY 10]. MacNamara is the general draper on the near, Barrack-Silver St corner – later owned by the Melody sisters, then Pat and Beatrice Hayes and now Brendan Galvin. However, the old building was demolished in 1995 and a handsome new one erected on the site. The National bank opened opposite on the Silver-Queen/Mitchel St corner in 1836 with Thaddeus O'Shea as manager. John O'Brien, butcher, and his wife Margaret lived at No. 41 in 1901. It is now O'Halloran's, undertakers.

The stretch of cobble stones at the entrance to each street slopes away to the gulleys to take care of surface water drainage.

9 (*opposite, below*) James (Jimmy) Mackey's bar and grocery at No. 1 Silver Street disappeared forever when it was demolished to make way for an extension to the expanding Bank of Ireland in 1979. Jimmy was an urban councillor 1965-79 and as its chairman figures in the Castle story on page 41. Previous owners included Michael Haugh, Secretary of Nenagh branch of the Land League and later the town's sanitary officer. Before that it was the retail outlet for Brindley's Happy Grove flour mill at Dolla.

10 Joseph Starr (1869-1922) moved his tailoring business from No. 26 Queen/Mitchel St [NY 38] across the street to No. 10 in 1907. His three sons, Michael, Thomas and Joe went to London to train as tailors. Michael opened in Portumna, Thomas emigrated to New York, and Joe (in picture)) continued on the business in Nenagh.

No. 10 is now the longest surviving of the original handsome frontages in the street. The tiles at the entrance were put down by Delaneys of Pound/Sarsfield St. The Starr & Sons signboard, described in a Foras Forbatha survey as 'Edwardian', carries the name of the maker – Brooks Thomas, Dublin.

In front of the shop in this 1930s picture are: Joe, with daughter Alice (now Ryan, Islandbawn) in his arms; his wife Margaret (née Ryan), and their children, (l to r) Joe, who continues the drapery business in No. 10; Johnny, Curraheen, and Michael, do.

11 Is this what Castle/Pearse Street will look like when the ESB and telephone cables are put underground?

Adam Hodgins is trading at No. 13, formerly Martha Byron's drapery, which he bought for £450 in a keenly-contested auction in 1885. He acquired James McCutcheon's (No.s 11 & 12) in 1893. [NY 21] The three were converted into a unified elegant shop with carved consoles and sun canopy, in the 1930s. The upper storey of No. 11 was the office of William Hodgins, solicitor, son of Adam.

The whole premises were demolished in 1992 after the retirement of Reggie (grandson of Adam) and Joan Hodgins: their drapery, **12** (*opposite, above*), was the epitome of elegance. It was replaced by a new block which now houses branches of the Supermacs restaurant and the Trustee Savings Bank chains.

13 (*below*) 58 Castle/Pearse St (now Omer Travel) was the retail outlet for Ryan's flour mill in Riverston off the Dublin road on the town side of the bridge over the Nenagh river. It was managed by John M. Ryan until his death in 1923. Most rural mills had outlets in the town – Brindleys, Dolla, already referred to on page 17, Bolands, Ballinaclough, and Clerhihans, Clarianna, both in Barrack/Kenyon St.

John M. Ryan was son of Thomas Ryan (1846-1917) who was a justice of the peace, Town Commissioner, and is described as 'Farmer and Mill Owner' in the contest for Nenagh division in the first County Council elections, 1899. He was defeated by seven votes, 351-344, by Martin Corbett, draper, Castle St. After a bitter battle, characterised by extensive press statements and letters, forthright personal attacks, allegations of distribution of porter (that being feared or claimed to be an effective form of bribery).

However, Thomas Ryan's political skill saw him co-opted, as one of two co-options allowed, by the inaugural Council.

14 The building on the corner of Peter/Kickham-Castle/Pearse Street has undergone more changes than any of its near neighbours. 1899 saw the Hodgins-owned multi-store block reduced to rubble by fire. A majestic building, incorporating No. 53 Castle/Pearse Street arose on the site [NY 19]. In 1926 that building, and Days at No. 52, were merged in a reconstruction to create the Munster and Leinster Bank. 'As regards the exterior', reported the *Nenagh Guardian*, 'the new portion of the front has been constructed of cast concrete blocks designed to give a simple and dignified effect, this object has been furthered by the construction of a new cornice round the whole building in the same material'.

The picture shows that 1926 bank in an early stage of demolition in 1979 [NY 17] to make way for one of the town's first buildings of non-traditional design.

15 & 16 This stoned-lined well (*below*) was uncovered during the AIB building project of 1979. Its exact location can be seen in context in the picture above, taken from O'Rahilly St. The wall on the left is the rear of the former North Tipperary Club (now Dún Mhuire) whose well it was. The gap left by the demolished bank allows a view of the upper storey of Nolan's public house. To the right of the gap is the rear of Gerard and Josie Irvine's shop and residence (now SPAR). Considerable excitement was generated when the well was sunk in the 1880s for, as the excavations reached a depth of thirty feet, large quantities of thick oil began to ooze in from the side 'which on a light being applied immediately ignited'.

17 (*opposite, above*) Another tranquil long view of **Castle/Pearse Street** between the Dublin Road corner and the Market Cross. Boland's ass-drawn bakery van has a contingent of young boys in attendance – Thomas Boland & Sons was advertising as 'The People's Bakery', 2 Barrack/Kenyon St, in 1908.

The signboard 'St. John' is legible on the shop at the extreme right of the picture. Widower Robert St. John, a watchmaker, lived here in 1901 with his daughters Margaret, Harriett and Edith.

18 (*opposite, below*) is the same shop trading as Ewings. William Ewing, watchmaker, worked with St. John and later took over the business. The gold leaf lettering, clock, barometer, and shutters which were put up every evening, were the landmarks of this traditional shop front for decades. At the door is owner Eileen (Dotney) Ewing with Florence Brown, Islandbawn. The Ewing ownership terminated with the death of Dotney in 1996.

19 (*above*) **At Dublin Road Corner c.1957.** The addresses in brackets are their current ones. **Back** (l to r): James Meagher, Sarsfield St (Nenagh); Eddie Clifford, Knockanpierce (England); Jer Ryan, MacDonagh St (England); Michael O'Brien, do. (Dublin); Frank O'Keeffe, Emmet Place (Nenagh); Denis Butler, MacDonagh St (Nenagh); Jimmy Butler, do. (Dublin); Jim Tierney, Rossa Place (USA); Michael Ryan, MacDonagh St (England); Tony Grace, Friar St (Nenagh); Malachy Cardiff, Sarsfield St; Seamie Hall, Silver St (Co. Laois); **Front:** Donal Flannery, Mitchel St; Paddy Shoer, St. Joseph's Park (Nenagh); Danny Mohilly, MacDonagh St (Nenagh); Sean Ryan, do. (England) (standing behind); Michael O'Meara, MacDonagh St (kneeling beside him); Tomás Ryan, do. (England) (behind dog); Sean and Eamon Carey, MacDonagh St. (Clonmel and Dublin respectively).

Dan Murphy is at the door of 39 Castle/Pearse St opposite (now the Magic Scissors hairdressers).

20 From the air in 1933

One for the magnifying glass!
This fine picture takes in Castle/ Pearse St, Pound/Sarsfield St, and Cudville/Ashe Road where greenfield sites abound – notably the hilly hollows (a cut-away quarry) and site of St Mary's Secondary School on the right, and on the left where the Scouts Hall and post office are now located. The only development in this mid-nineteenth century road are the 1906 terrace of fourteen UDC houses named for Wolfe Tone, and the ex-Servicemen's Club House and war memorial of the late 1920s. At the top of the road Mary Spain's field (now Cudville Green) and the fields on both sides of Richmond/St Conlan's Road are active farmland.

The surviving small tower (there were two originally) of the castle gatehouse is well defined as are the numerous and varied structures in the back yards.

21 This is a pre-1911 view of Upper Castle/Pearse Street – before John Swanton moved his business from across the road at No. 24 [NY 20] to Patrick Carroll's premises shown above at No. 47. Carroll had a grocery, seed merchant business and cycle depot.

William Harkness, trading at No. 46 in 1893, alert to the fact that the town was about to get a piped water scheme, informed his potential customers (by an advertisement in the *Nenagh Guardian*) that he had in stock 'newest sanitary and general water fittings suitable for new water schemes'. Harknesses were also plumbers and gunmakers.

Jeremiah O'Brien, grocer and spirit merchant, traded next door at No. 45. The three premises are now incorporated in the Castle Hyperstore.

Two unusual views of Nenagh Castle

22 (*above*) This picture reiterates what is already clear from the aerial view on pages 24-5 that the evolving town encroached very much on the castle's space. This view shows the back yard of No. 44, the tower in the foreground is the remaining one of a pair which guarded the main entrance from Bachelor's Walk/O'Rahilly Street.

23 (*left*) This is a unique picture. Artist Lancelot Bayly, Bayly Farm, Ballinaclough, pitched his easel at the top of the Dublin Road and painted the castle keep through the break in the streetscape which had occurred as a result of the burning of Gill's Printing Works at No. 38 and of Mrs Mary Nolan's licenced premises at No. 37 by the Black and Tans in November 1920 during the War of Independence.

24 (*opposite, above*) A fine view of Summerhill before many residents surfaced in the morning. Note the tasteful gas light in the left foreground. The stone wall near it is the entrance to 'Summerville'. The bar & grocery opposite is owned by T(om) Murphy, a Constable in the RIC.

25 (*opposite, below*) **'Summerville'**
This eighteenth-century Georgian house was demolished in the late 1960s to make way for the development of the Christian Brothers schools and monastery. It was the home of the town's landlord, Peter Holmes, Jun. and his family until his death in 1843, then that of his widow, Mary Augusta (née Postle), who married Major John Hamilton Dundas as her second husband. Next came Major Edgar Waller and, finally, Willie Hodgins, Solicitor, and his family.

26 (*above*) Powell Bros bar and grocery, with Mrs Bobby Powell (née Josephine Bourke) at the doorway. Bobby (Robert) and Tommy were brothers. The latter had a business in Silver St. The shop's front dates from the 1930s and has been impeccably maintained since. The grocery end of the business faded out once the supermarkets came on the scene in the 1960s. However, the bar fittings and furniture have not been replaced.

27 The Military Barracks was built in 1832. The builder was John Hanly, Summerhill, who has left us a fine legacy of his later work in the gaol and courthouse. The main block facing the barrack square had accommodation for commissioned officers in the centre and for non-commissioned officers in the two side wings. The ball alley at the water tower end is a later addition. Missing from the picture is the barrack master's dwelling – a detached building (still standing) to the right. The barracks was garrisoned by regiments of the British Army almost continually until 1922 when the North Staffordshire Regiment departed after the Irish Free State came into being. The Irish army occupied it for two years – 1922-4.

Its sole occupant now is the F(órsa) C(osanta) Á(itiúla) (Local Defence Force). For years its rooms were utilised as office accommodation for local headquarters of government departments – the Office of Public Works, Labour, and Social Welfare. The square was a popular venue for fund-raising bazaars in the last century and carnivals in the 1930s-'50s.

The reinforced water tower in the adjoining field was completed for Nenagh UDC in 1959.

28 (*left*) One of big rooms in the central building; the fireplace has the insignia of the reigning King in 1832 – William IV, Queen Victoria's uncle and predecessor.

29 (*above*) A single-storey
block housed the kitchen and
(dining) mess; a similar
separate block in line with it
had accommodation for four
horses and their handlers.

30 (*middle*) The unique ovens
from the kitchen.

31 (*left*) The stable dividers, hay
baskets and water troughs. All
had withstood the years of neglect
up to the 1980s when these
pictures were taken.

32 Peter/Kickham Street: Another early-morning picture of the 1890s. The seated figure of Justice looks down on the turf creels making their way to the turf market then held where the Town Hall was built in 1889. She was removed in 1896 when her weight was found have done extensive damage to the pediment. The first court in the new courthouse was the Spring Assizes of 1844.

A lone gaslight lights the square and street. Dominant on the left is the corn and wool store then owned by John F. Tumpane. Successive owners were Frank R. Maloney and Frank McGrath. After several years as Ryan's fuel and hardware store the building was refurbished as Nenagh Credit Union offices (1996).

The premises of Michael Quirke, Pawnbroker, on the right, are readily identifiable by the traditional pawnbroker's sign of three brass spheres.

33 (*opposite, right*) Jamesy The Monument [NY 49] oversees the final stage of the annual **Corpus Christi procession**. The crowds face the courthouse steps, transformed to an altar with banner and floral decorations, in this early 1950s Jack Ryan picture.

The former Presbyterian church of 1906 has undergone little architectural change to its facade in its transition to the Public Health offices in 1940 and Motor Taxation Offices, 1972. O'Riordan's house and Jerry's Yard are now replaced by the Ulster Bank. The shed area between the yard and former church now houses the SIPTU office and McLoughlin's hardware.

Chumneys, with the VEC offices in part; Jim O'Sullivan's public house (1946), Marjorie Healy's laundry depot (now Murnane's dental surgery) are all visible. Irvines' grocery and bacon shop has its sun canopy open, while on the far side of Castle/Pearse Street Frank Flannery's auction rooms are in the former Renehan's drapery.

33 (contd) Ciss Maguire, N.T., Convent primary school, and two of the flower girls are in the foreground left. Among the canopy carriers are Bro.s Stapleton, left, and Hayes, right, facing the camera. Paddy Chumney, marshal, is close behind.

Sergeants Cox and George Cardiff flank Gardaí Jacksie Murphy, Dinny Finnan, Michael Brennan, –, with Pat Ahearne, Tom O'Connor and Sgt McLoughlin behind. The officers are Supt. Barney Deignan, front, and Inspector John Nolan, behind. [NY 45, 48]

34 (*above*) In 1960-1 Nenagh Urban District Council erected seven houses on a vacant plot of ground between the Rialto cinema and Hanly's Lane/Place. They were blessed by Right Rev. Monsignor Michael Hamilton, P.P., V.G., in March 1961. Included in above picture are (l to r): Sean T. O'Neill, Town Clerk; Tom Brophy, Co. Secretary; Denis Gleeson, Rent Collector, Silver St; Micheál Corrigan, UDC, Mitchel St (now Tyone); John Ryan, MCC, UDC, St Patrick's Tce; Mary Quigley, Pound/Sarsfield St; Frankie O'Donnell, UDC, Silver Street; Dr Mary Ryan, M.O., Nenagh Dispensary; Mick Bonfield, Pound/Sarsfield St; Elsie Mitchell, St. Joseph's Park.

35 (*below*) Included are Eileen Bowler, Hanly's Place; Eileen Cooney, St. Flannan's St; John McLoughlin, Wolfe Tone Tce, *Nenagh Guardian* reporter; Mick Bonfield; John Matt Dooley, Postmaster; Brian Tansey, Town Surveyor; Rev. J. Hogan, C.C.; Denis Gleeson; Clrs Joe Devane, Pound/Sarsfield St, M. Corrigan, J. Ryan and F. O'Donnell.

36 (*left*) Seen here watching the actual blessing ceremony, with St. Mary's new secondary school in the background, are Michael Geaney, Knockanpierce, with son Seán; John Darmody, Silver St; Sean T. O'Neill; Matt Collison, Moneygall, builder of the scheme, and Mrs Collison.

37 At an inspection of **Nenagh's new sewerage treatment plant**, Birr/Bulfin Road, were Councillor Dan O'Keeffe, St. Flannan's St; Sean T. O'Neill, Town Clerk; Councillor Micheál Corrigan; Michael J. O'Sullivan, Consulting Engineer; Councillor John Ryan; Brian Tansey, Town Surveyor; Councillor Joe Devane.

The scheme went to Messrs C. Dodd, Bray, whose tender of £53,000 was accepted in April 1959. However, by February 1962 the cost had risen to £76,000 as up to five extensions had been added in the interim. The extensions brought areas like Tyone, William St and Clare St into the scheme.

38 The plant included a pump house and percolating filters, and humus tanks and sludge beds (*above*). What sewage remained after filtering drained into the nearby Nenagh river. This plant was replaced with a new, upgraded one on a nearby site in the 1980s.

39 Nenagh's ultra-modern 575-seater **Rialto Cinema** opened in 1946. [NY 57] It was the town's second purpose-built cinema as The New Ormond had opened in Summerhill the previous year. Seen here in the projection room are Rialto projectionists Jimmy McCarthy (2nd from left) and Christy Sherlock (extreme right), both of Knockanpierce. The cinema closed in the mid-1970s and became, firstly, Kilroy's (Tullamore) furniture store and, secondly, Sheahan's builders' providers.

40 (*left*) The keep had the curtain wall intact, and substantial remains of the gatehouse upper storey were extant, when this drawing was made by Austin Cooper, Dundrum, in 1784.

41 (*right*) The demarcation line of the 'crown' of 1861 is easily discernable. This was put on by Lant Ryan, builder, Newport, when Bishop Michael Flannery of Killaloe, then resident in Nenagh, acquired the ruin with the intention of using the keep as the belfry for the cathedral he planned to build in the adjoining field. It added about twenty-five feet to the keep's height. However, the original wall-walk was not interfered with.

Note the projecting bondstones which joined the keep and former curtain wall.

In time the view through to the Dublin road corner was obscured by the advent of buildings in Falvey's Lane/Church View and trees in the Castle field.

The full story of the 'crown' is recounted in *Walkabout Nenagh*, pages 137-8. *Nenagh Castle, chronology and architecture*, has more detail on the interior features.

42 (*above*) In 1971 a meitheal to clean up the castle keep in preparation for its re-opening to the public was organised by the Castle Restoration Committee. This eight-person working party had been elected at a public meeting in December 1970. A few Saturday mornings saw the deep layer of dirt removed from the concrete floor and stairs. The workers were: **Back** (l to r): Johnny Shoer, Sallygrove, with son Pádraig; Tom McGrath, Whitewalls (cttee); Michael Bergin, Cudville; – ; Martin Lawlor, Birr/Bulfin Rd and O'Hara's Tyone mills; Jimmy Mackey, Silver Street (Chairman of Nenagh UDC); Donal Murphy, Tyone (committee chairman); Nancy Murphy, Tyone; Margaret McGrath (now Bent), Whitewalls; Eamonn De Stafort, Shannonside Tourism and Silvermines. **Front:** Eimear Burke, Gortlands (cttee); Aidan Bent, Gortlandroe; Noel Ryan, St. Patrick's Terrace (cttee); Catherine McGrath (now Tierney, Limerick); Eileen McGrath; Jane McGrath (now Flannery, Cork) all of Whitewalls.

The project was brought to a conclusion with the erection of the coats of arms of the fifteen leading families in this area during the period 1200-1600, painted by another meitheal of local artists; the re-publication of 'Nenagh Castle and Manor' by Dermot F. Gleeson and Harold Leask; and the official opening of the keep to the public on 28 June 1971 with a pageant telling its story.

43 (*below, left*) The Butler coat of arms unveiled by Jimmy Mackey, Chairman, Nenagh UDC.

44 (*below, right*) Donal Murphy, chairman of the Restoration committee, and George Butler, President of the Butler Society, also participated in the unveiling ceremony preceding the re-opening.

45 Once the floor and stairs had been cleaned the wall walk became accessible. For those with a head for heights the masonry work of 1861, which includes mock crenellations (*left*), could be viewed at close quarters.

46 There was a fine view from each of the windows, and from vantage points on the wall walk one could see the sandstone surrounds and other features of the fireplaces, windows and (*right*) the probable door opening leading to the garderobe (medieval lavatory).

47 (*right*) The little compartments in this recess may have been for altar vessels in an area set aside as an oratory.

48 (*above*) **St. Mary's of the Rosary**, which celebrated the centenary of its opening this year (1996) [NY 71, 72], is shown flanked by the church's two older neighbours – the keep of Nenagh's thirteenth-century Norman Castle, and St. Mary's Church of Ireland church (1860). This fine picture was taken from the site of the later Boys National School.

49 (*opposite, above*) **The church's chancel/sanctuary and altar pre-1912.** The altar was donated in 1904 by Martin and Susan Corbett, 47 Castle/Pearse St. It was made for them by the firm of James Sharpe, Dublin. The walls below the stained glass window are plain plaster except for two small murals.

50 (*opposite, below*) The same view after the insertion of the mosaic and marble work of 1912 for which the plans were prepared by Messrs Ashlin and Coleman.

> The principal feature … is a mixture of rich coloured marble, with gold mosaic, and besides these are additions in marble to the Altar. Midway on each side of the chancel is a heavy moulding of white stone inlaid with mosaic and three pedestals and canopies resting on angel heads and coloured marble supports, containing statues in stone, the space between being filled with designs in richest mosaic.
>
> … There are two subjects elaborately treated in picture, viz. the Assumption and the Coronation of the Blessed Virgin. … All the reveals of the windows (seventeen in number) are treated in gold mosaic and the spandrils over the arches are decorated in the same way. (*Nenagh Guardian*, Jan. 1912).

In preparation for the new decoration all the plaster had to be removed and the walls stripped down to the stone and re-covered with cement. This was done by Messrs Sheridan, Newbridge.

Bishop Michael Fogarty donated £200 and sent on the bequest of Captain Daniel Flannery (a native of Kilruane who had died in the U.S.A.) which totalled £528. The overall cost was £1,900.

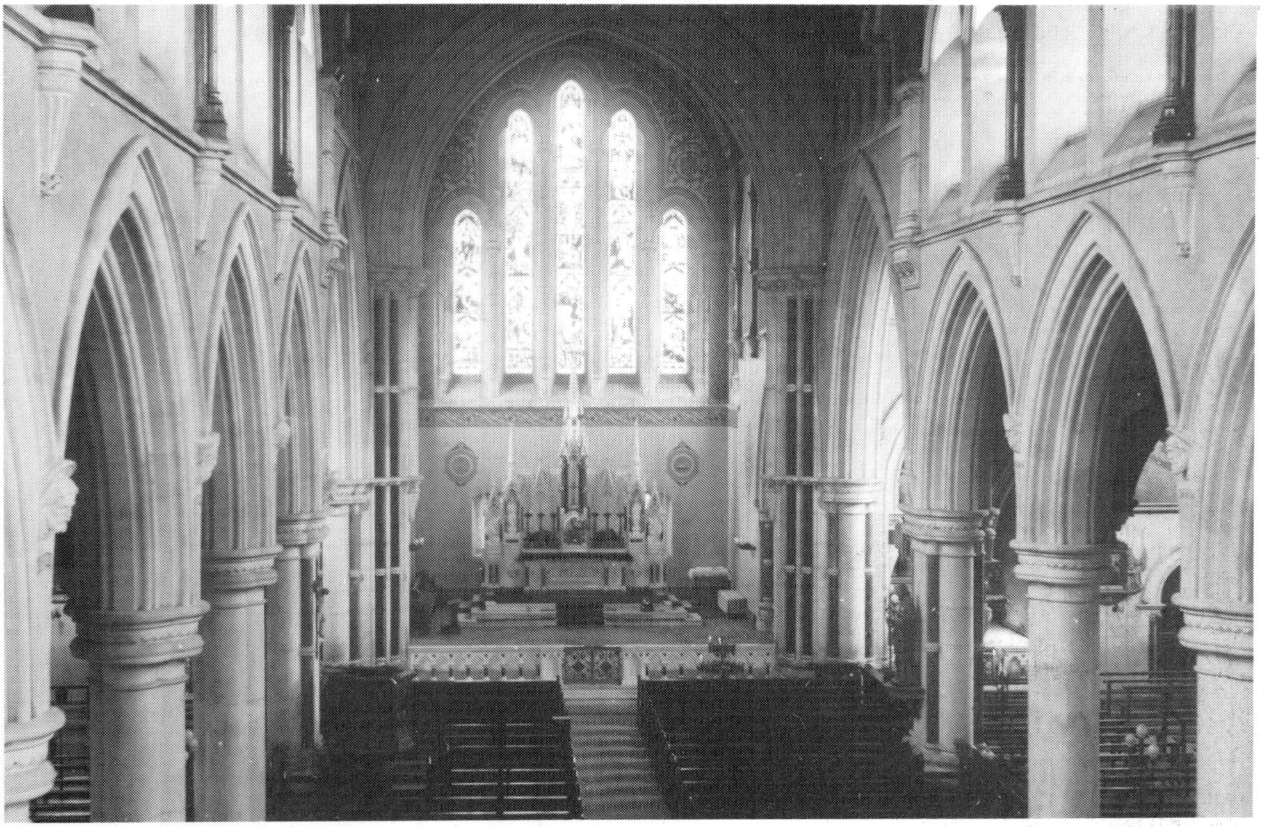

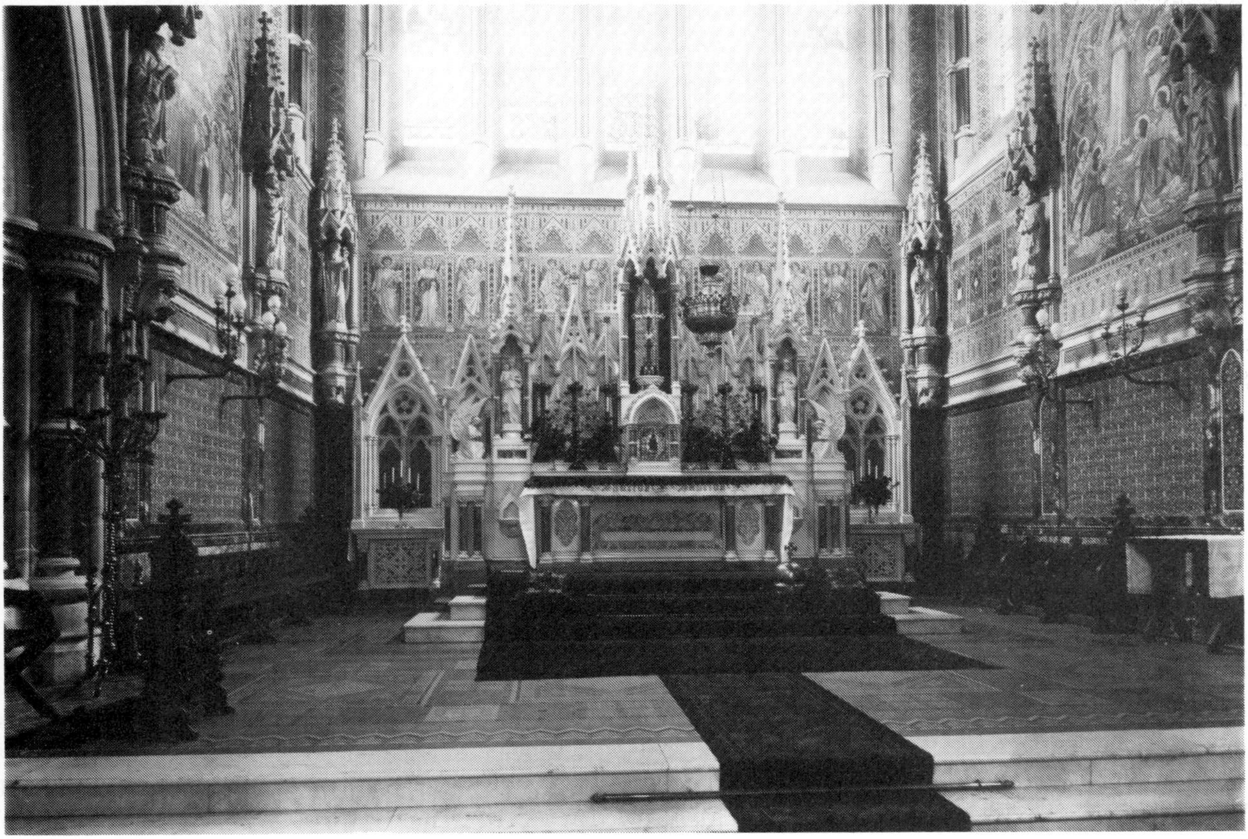

51 Cudville/Ashe Road has two of Nenagh's pieces of public art – the bronze figure of the postman on a bicycle on the post office wall, and the representation of the Holy Family (*above*), cast in concrete, by the well-known Dublin-based artist, Gary Trimble, which is located in the grounds of St. Mary's Secondary school. Its original position, as of 1957, was in front of the assembly hall (it is discernable in picture no. 36, page 35), but later additions to the school necessitated its re-location to its present position near the tennis courts.

In 1981 the **(Nenagh) Guardian's** centuries-old system of typesetting words in hot metal was replaced by computerised typesetting. [NY196] Paste-up pages, negatives and aluminium plates replaced the chases of metal type. The in-house work now ceases after the plate-making stage – these are then sent to the *Limerick Leader* for printing.

52 (*above*) Liam Bourke, printer, putting the last chase of the last *Guardian* printed in Nenagh into position on the Twin Cossar printing machine.

53 (*right*) Four chases (made up of columns of hot metal 'slugs') in their beds. Rollers distributed ink on to them and the newsprint, feeding in from a large roller (as shown above), was then brought into contact with the inked chase. The electricity-driven Twin Cossar, which was installed in the 1950s, could produce about 1,500 copies of folded sixteen-page newspapers per hour.

54 (*left*) Until 1982 harness-maker and saddler Paddy O'Sullivan was a familiar figure at the window of No. 45 Pound/Sarsfield St. Paddy came from Killarney in the late 1920s to work with Lar White, harness-maker and saddler at 22 Queen/Mitchel St. Whites closed down around 1959, and Paddy commenced business in his own house. He died in 1983, at the fine age of 84 – having been the last person in the town to practise this skilled trade.

55 (*opposite, below*) **Michael Geaney outside his coach factory** at No.s 34-5 Barrack/Kenyon Street (beside what is now Micheál Ó Coileáin's confectionery). (l to r): Michael Geaney, owner; John Geaney, son, smith; Dan Maloney, carpenter; Tommy McMahon, painter; Billy Watson, smith; Jimmy Jones.

No.s 34 & 35 had a long tradition of coach and carriage building. Cork native Michael Geaney took over the Jones establishment here in the 1920s. He died in 1939.

1995 also saw this entire premises demolished and replaced by a new one, now Valette Insurances, as part of the urban renewal scheme, 1994-7. That plan provides for incentives by way of tax relief and rates remissions for work carried out on buildings in seven areas in the town designated by the Minister for the Environment.

56 In Corneille's Bacon Factory 1923-4, 16-17 Castle/Pearse St [NY 13, 14] (later the Ormond Garage and now the Agricultural Credit Corporation branch). **Back** (l to r): Michael Ryan, Dublin Rd/MacDonagh St; – Pike, Limerick; Jimmy Meagher, Monsea. **Front:** Tom Guilfoyle, Tullaheady; Ned Riordan, Birr/Bulfin Rd; Patrick (Sonny) Hackett, Silver Street; Matt Sheary, Ballincur, Silvermines; Johnny Martin, Birr/Bulfin Rd; – Blennerhassett, Kerry.

Corneilles killed and cured 25 pigs per week, all bought in Nenagh and Borrisokane markets, approximately 40 stone, at £4 to £5 each. Best rashers were sold at 1*s* 8*d* (8.5p) per pound weight. Mr Pike, the bacon curer, came by train from Limerick every Monday and stayed in O'Meara's Hotel until Friday.

57 (*above*) Two generations of Hogan blacksmiths figure in this picture: William Hogan (in the doorway) and his son Edward (Neddy) tending to the horse outside the Hogan forge in Dublin Rd/MacDonagh St. The man alongside is probably named Quinn from Bourne's Lane and owner of the horse. The other men remain unidentified. Mrs Nonie Slattery is in the doorway of her house next to the forge.

The forge was a notable 'educational institution' in that people dropped in and discussed current affairs. Dan Morrissey, Nenagh's first Government Minister (1948-51) told *Guardian* reporter Patricia Feehily that he learned more in Hogan's forge than anywhere else.

William Hogan was active in the Trade and Labour Association and Town Tenants Association. He was also a member of Nenagh UDC from 1920 to the mid-1930s. He died in 1931, aged 65 years. Neddy Hogan was secretary of Nenagh Literary Institute for over fifty years – almost up to the time of his death in 1963.

58 (*opposite, above*) Do It Yourself by a travelling family at the Cloughjordan-Dublin roads junction in 1982.

59 (*opposite below*) Bill Cavanagh, 3 MacDonagh Terrace, in his forge in River Lane/Keating Place. He worked here until close to 90 years of age. The diamond-paned windows came from the workhouse in Tyone upon its demolition in 1935. Sean Quinn, Stafford St and Tyone, has retained the windows in refurbishing the premises; it is now his son John's antiques restoration workshop and salesroom.

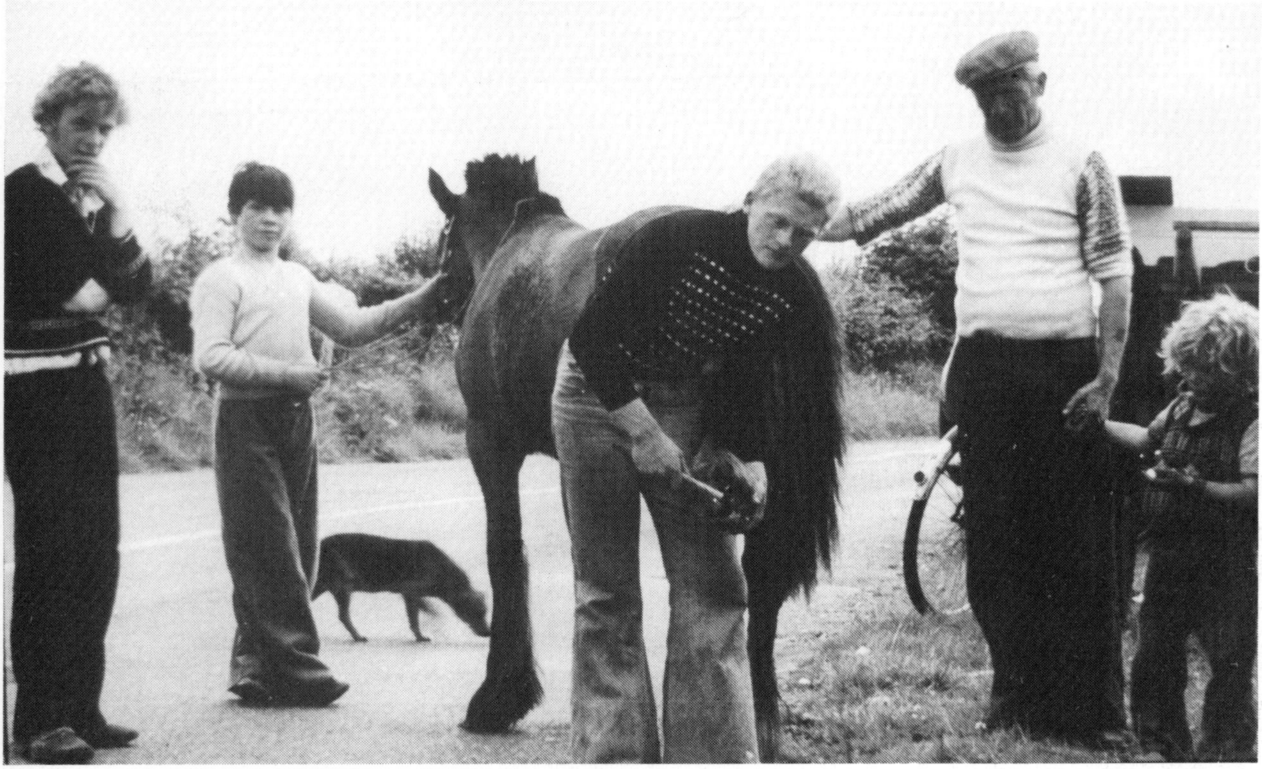

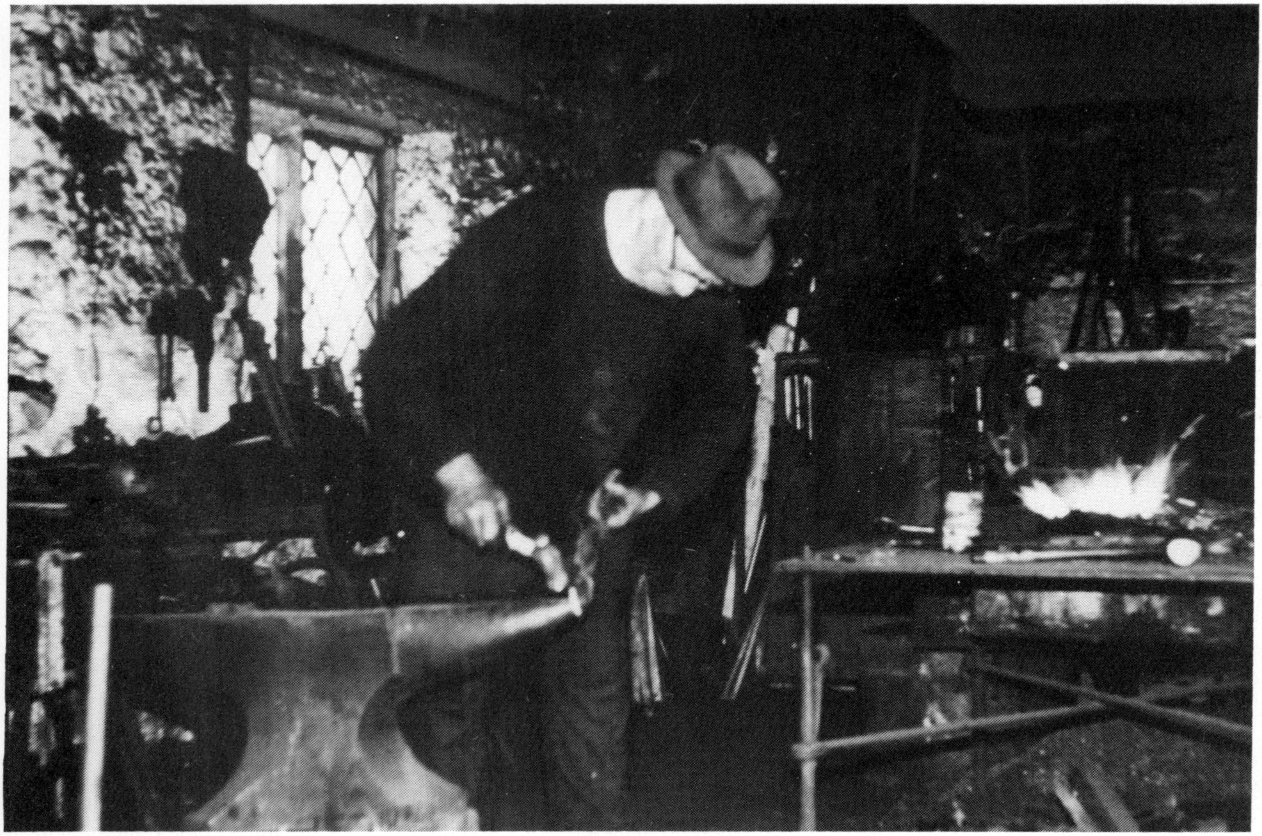

60 Michael O'Kennedy received a handsome send-off from Nenagh Urban District Council on 21 February 1981 upon taking up office as Irish Commissioner to the European Economic Community. **Back** (l to r): Councillors Billy Bailey, Fianna Fáil (1979-85), Tobar Mhuire; Tom Ryan, Fine Gael (1979-), Rathnaleen; Tony McCormack, Town Clerk (1969); John McGinley, County Manager (1978); Councillors Michael O'Meara, Independent (1967-82), Melrose, and Noel Clifford, Labour (1974-85, '93-), Silver Street. **Front:** Councillor Joseph O'Connor, Ind (1979-) Tyone, Chairman; Mrs Breda O'Kennedy, Gortlandroe; Michael O'Kennedy, T.D., (UDC 1974-9); John Ryan, Lab (1960-), TD, MCC, St Patrick's Terrace; Councillors Dr Maureen Carmody, Lab (1979-85), Stoney High, and Ger Ryan, FF (1967-), MCC, Mitchel Street. Donal Morrissey, Benedine, FG, is absent from the photograph. (*Dates = duration of membership/appointment*). [NY 53-7]

Michael O'Kennedy had been Minister for Finance in the Government led by Charles J. Haughey from December 1979 following over two years as Minister for Foreign Affairs under Jack Lynch as Taoiseach. On his one entry into urban politics, his Fianna Fáil machine put him at the head of the poll with an all-time record 575 votes – 21% of the total cast for seventeen candidates. That was in 1974. Four of his colleagues from that 1974-9 Council were still in office: Cllrs J. Ryan, M. O'Meara, N. Clifford and G. Ryan. Cllr O'Connor, though non-party, was Chairman in 1981 by virtue of a unique Nenagh convention which gave him, as second to be elected in 1979, office in the second year of the Council's life. [see *Walkabout Nenagh*, pp. 11-13]

The O'Kennedy commissionership lasted just fourteen months. He returned in February 1982 in an attempt to win a second seat for FF in Tipperary North in the second of three general elections within eighteen months which convulsed national politics. He was elected but his FF colleague, Michael Smith, lost his seat. O'Kennedy resigned the commissionership in March.

61 Extreme left: 'My temporary number in Brussels is …' **Extreme right:** 'Now I remember Ned Kennedy telling me …'

62 We're staying put: Cllrs G. Ryan & B. Bailey with Gerry McLoughlin, *The Guardian* reporter.

63 Off the record: T. McCormack, Maria Marron, *Midland Tribune* and the short-lived *Nenagh Tribune*, Michael Maguire, Hotel Ormond.

64 The new general hospital at Nenagh was opened by Sean T. O'Kelly, T.D., Minister for Local Government and Public Health (later President of Ireland, 1945-59) on 30 September 1936. It replaced the former workhouse infirmary [NY 76, 131] which had been providing a county-wide medical, maternity and surgical service for Tipperary (North Riding) since 1923. Seven-eighths of the £62,000 cost came from the Sweepstake Fund – the first new hospital to benefit from this financial source, which had an impact similar to today's National Lottery.

The Minister is seen second from left, with Tim Sheehy, MCC, Chairman of the Tipperary North Board of Health reading the address. Michael Kelly, Chairman, Nenagh UDC, is behind the Minister, with Sean T. O'Neill, Town Clerk, to his right in picture. Dr. A.D. Courtney, Co. Physician-Surgeon, is on the extreme front right. The architect, Vincent A. Kelly, Dublin, and the contractor, Samuel A. Phillips, Dublin, are also among the dignitaries.

65 (*left*) On the occasion of the visit of the Lord Abbot of Mount St. Joseph Monastery, Roscrea, to Nenagh's new hospital in the 1940s. (l to r): Sr Madeleine O'Donoghue, Matron; Sr Cronan Healy, retired teacher; Sr Bernadette Grey, laundry department; Sr Elizabeth Maxwell, Assistant Matron; Sr Columba Harty, nurse; Sr Concepta Keenan, nurse; Sr Joseph Mary Tumpane, convent staff; Dr James Walsh, House Officer; Dr A.D. Courtney, Co. Physician-Surgeon; Sr Gabriel O'Dwyer, nurse. **Front:** The Lord Abbott; –.

66 (*below*) In 1961 Dr A. D. (Louis) Courtney retired after forty-two years in the hospital. He was appointed M.O. to the workhouse infirmary in 1919 and County Physician-Surgeon when that infirmary was upgraded to Co. Hospital status in 1923. After the appointment of a County Surgeon in the early 1950s he continued as Co. Physician until 1961. His retirement was marked with a dinner and presentation. **Back** (l to r): Nurses Nora Ryan; Teresa Carey (now Treacy); Colleen Dwan (now Shelly); Evelyn O'Neill, Radiographer; Nurses Nancy O'Grady (now O'Brien); Mary Droney (now Collins); Kathleen Geraghty (née McKeogh); Maureen Moroney; Tess O'Donoghue (née Condon); Nancy Tynan (now Murphy); Mary Treacy (née O'Sullivan); Evelyn Murphy (née O'Donovan). **Front:** Peggy McGuire (now Jones), Clerical Officer; Breda O'Dea, Radiographer; Nurses Sally O'Connor (now O'Meara); Betty Costello; Dr A. D. Courtney; Nurses Julia O'Leary; Joan Murphy (now Moylan); Sally Moloney (now McGuigan); Maura Purcell (now Molumby), Clerk-Typist.

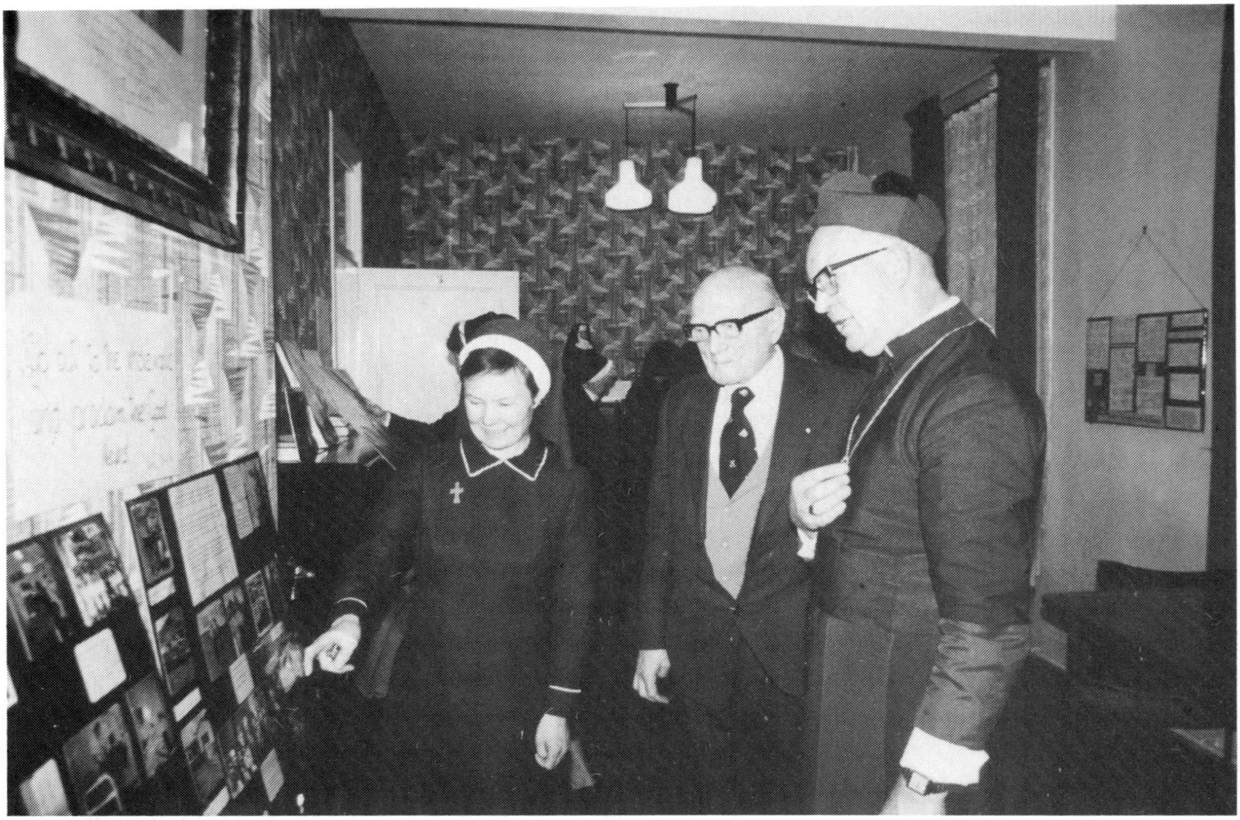

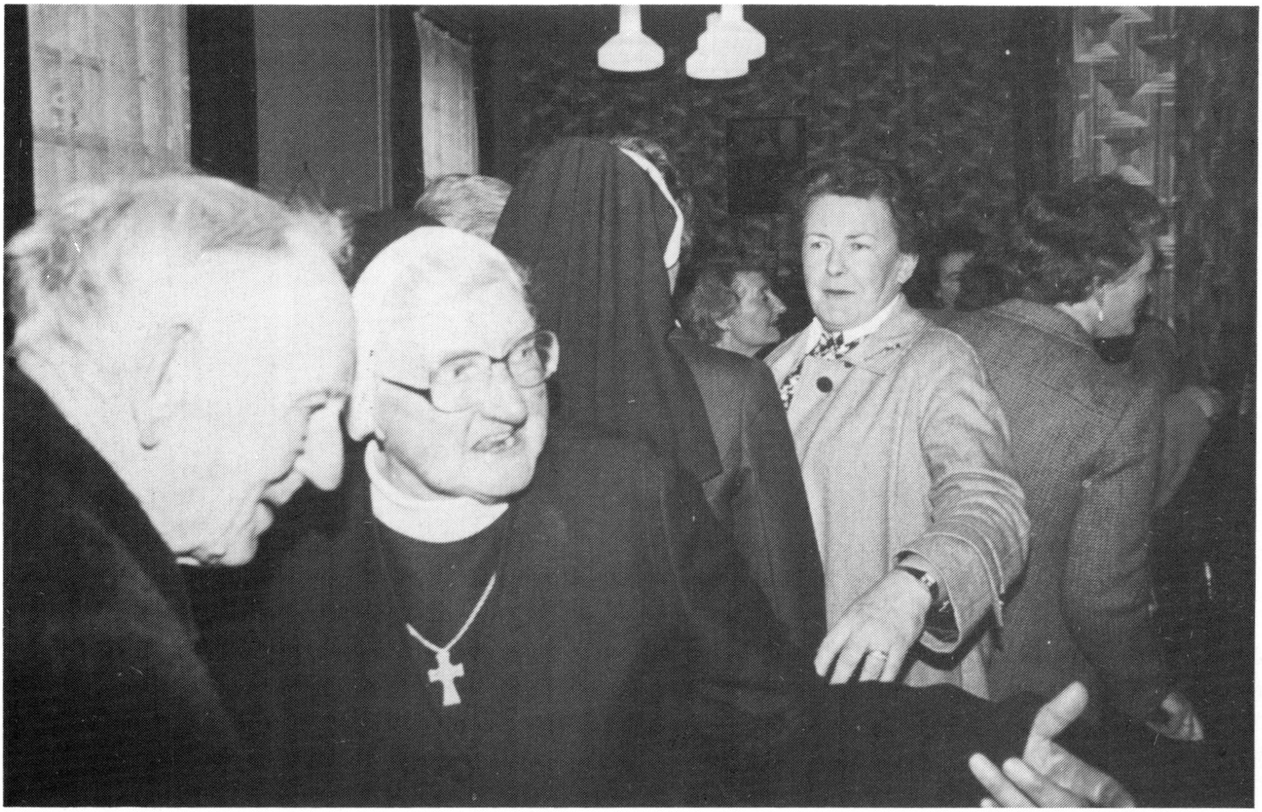

In 1982 the Sisters of Mercy celebrated the centenary of their appointment as nurses to Nenagh Poor Law Union workhouse. The celebrations extended to a special Mass in St John's, Tyone, an exhibition of photographs and documents, and a dinner for past and present hospital and convent staff.

67 (*opposite, above*) Sr Stephanie Murphy, Matron, with Dr A. D. Courtney, former Co. Physician, and Most Rev. Dr Michael Harty, Bishop of Killaloe. Sr Stephanie was the last member of the Sisters of Mercy to hold the post of Matron, as the Order discontinued the practice of holding senior administrative posts in acute hospitals when her term of office ended in 1983.

68 (*opposite, below*) It was a great occasion for renewing acquaintance with former colleagues. (in front) John O'Grady, ambulance driver (retired after forty-two years service in 1961), with Sr Annunciata Devane, retired Assistant Matron; (behind) Sr Bernard Quigley with Dr Meda Lehane (née O'Callaghan), a former house officer. In between them is Sally Gardiner, former theatre sister, and to their right is Nora Sheehy (née Callan, a former nurse).

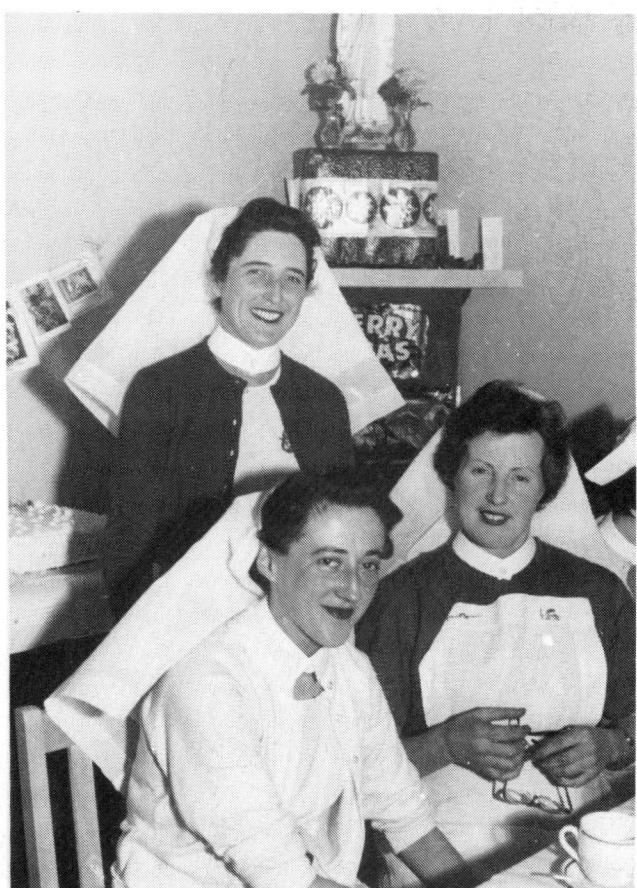

69 Christmas 1959 in the Nurses' Diningroom
Back: Mev Murphy, Tulla, Co. Clare (later Seymour).
Front: Maura Gaynor, Tyone, and Betty Costello, Cloughjordan.

In June 1982 staff from Nenagh hospital undertook a trolley push from Cork to Nenagh to raise funds for an ultra-sound machine. The estimated cost was £60,000, of which the Mid-Western Health Board undertook to pay half. Various individuals and voluntary groups also ran events and the target of £35,000 was within sight by early July. The machine, which is a non-invasive way of examining internal organs, was soon installed in the hospital.

Nenagh's brass band gave them a musical escort for the last leg of the journey on 19 June.

70 (*above, left*) passing through Wolfe Tone Terrace.

71 (*left*) The group at the end of the journey with the hospital in the background. **Back** (l to r): Sr Mary McInerney; Kieran Maguire, Attendant; Geraldine Quinlan (now Dunne), Domestic Attendant; (behind her) Michael Fogarty, clerical staff, Community Care, Kenyon Street; Gerry O'Rourke, Supplies Officer; (behind him) Michael Looney, Attendant; Noel Clifford, Attendant; D. Mulcahy's son. **Middle:** Nurses Mary Lanigan; Helena Ryan; Stephen Maguire; Alice Mulcahy, Nurse; Siobhán Keogh (now Burke), Domestic Attendant; Denis Mulcahy, Attendant; Nurse Breda Ryan. **Front:** Jimmy Starr, Attendant; Mary Sheahan (now Minogue), Administration.

Beside the ambulance are (*left*) Sean Kennedy, (*right*) Johnny McGrath, and two unidentified nurses.

A car and caravan was loaned to them by a local garage.

72 (*right*) Buckets of paper punts are amalgamated by Denis Mulcahy and Sr Mary McInerney.

73 A popular way of fund-raising in the pre-1950s was to hold a Garden Fête in the grounds of one of the Big Houses in the area. This picture of the early 1930s was taken on such an occasion – at Lord and Lady Dunalley's Kilboy House. It was probably more a fashion than a beauty contest. The group is a mix of contestants and spectators. **Back** (l to r): – ; Maureen O'Farrell, Scarriff & Nenagh, winner; – Mounsey. **Middle:** – ; – ; –; –; –; –; –. **Front:** Maureen Irvine, St Patrick's Tce, Nenagh; Molly Barry, Summerhill, Nenagh; Eileen Barry, do; – ; – ; – ; – ; Mrs Gordon Webb, Curraghbawn, Newtown.

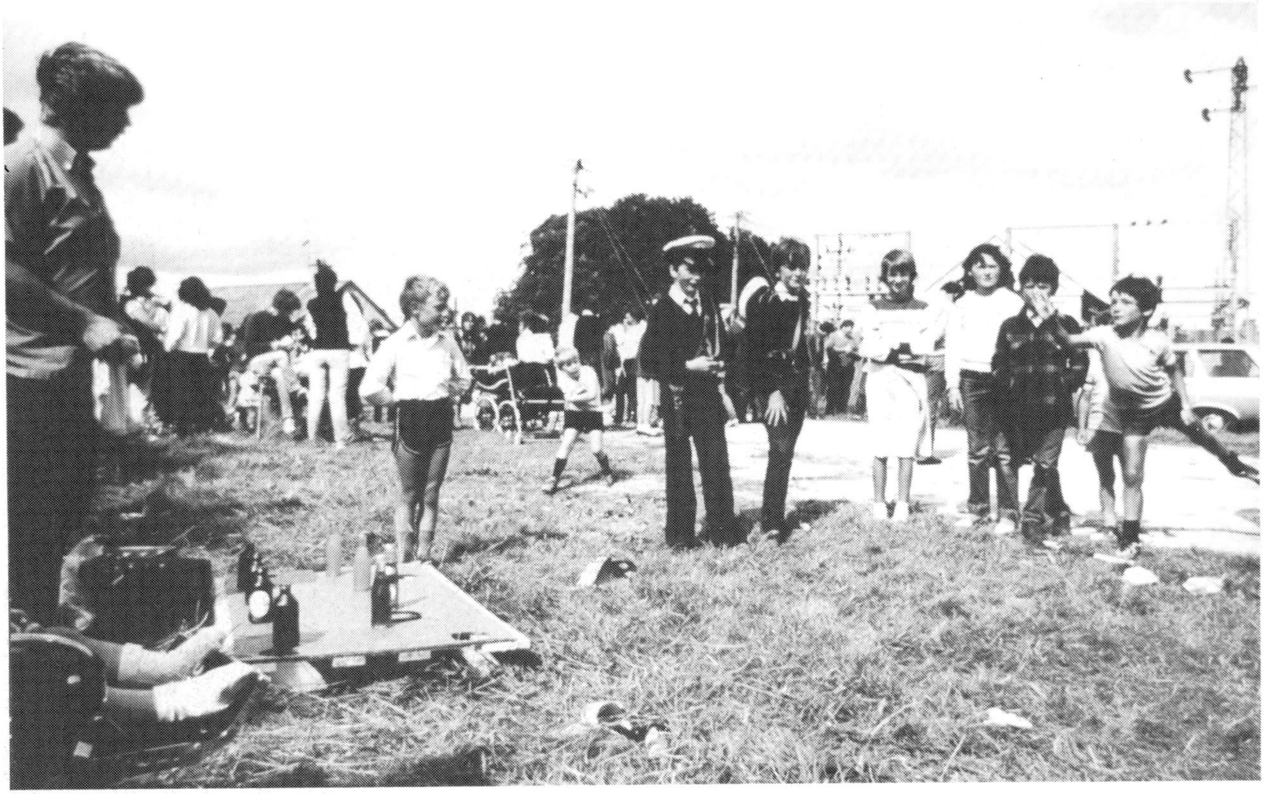

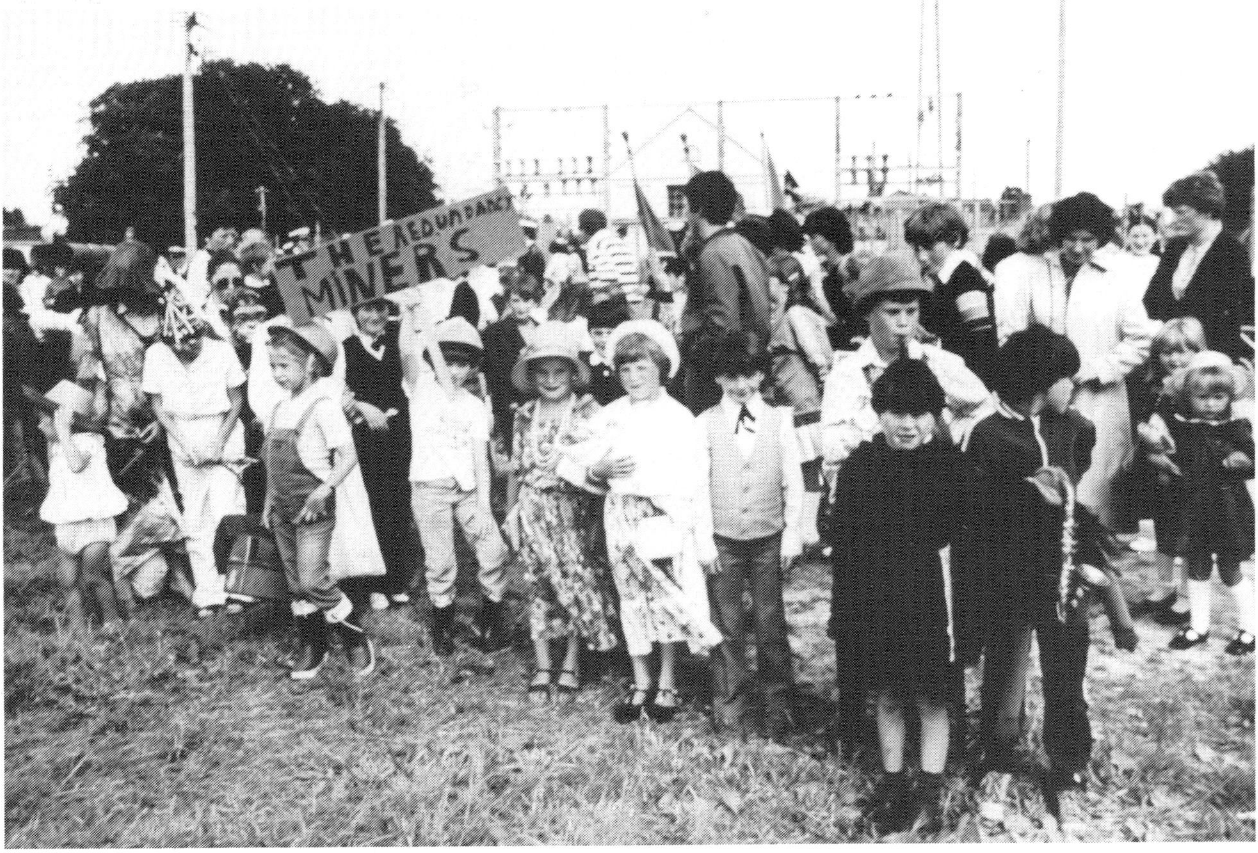
THE REDUNDANT
MINERS

Nenagh Ormond Rugby Club's second annual Field Day was held in their grounds, Tyone, on Sunday 8 August 1982. It had the usual attractions of wheel-of-fortune, ring throwing, fancy dress parade, and a ladies football match.

74 (*opposite, above*) Nenagh Brass Band was in attendance to lead the parade participants, provide a musical recital, and support an aspiring ring thrower in action.

75 (*opposite, below*) The newsmakers at local, national and international levels were reflected in the fancy dress entrants – the Choral Society's 'Hello Dolly' (pink dress & hat); the mooted closing of the Mogul mine at Silvermines, and the arrival of Charles' and Diana's first baby, Prince William.

76 (*above*) Johnny Whelan takes money from juvenile punters while Kevin Lewis, also a NORFC stalwart, minds the blind side.

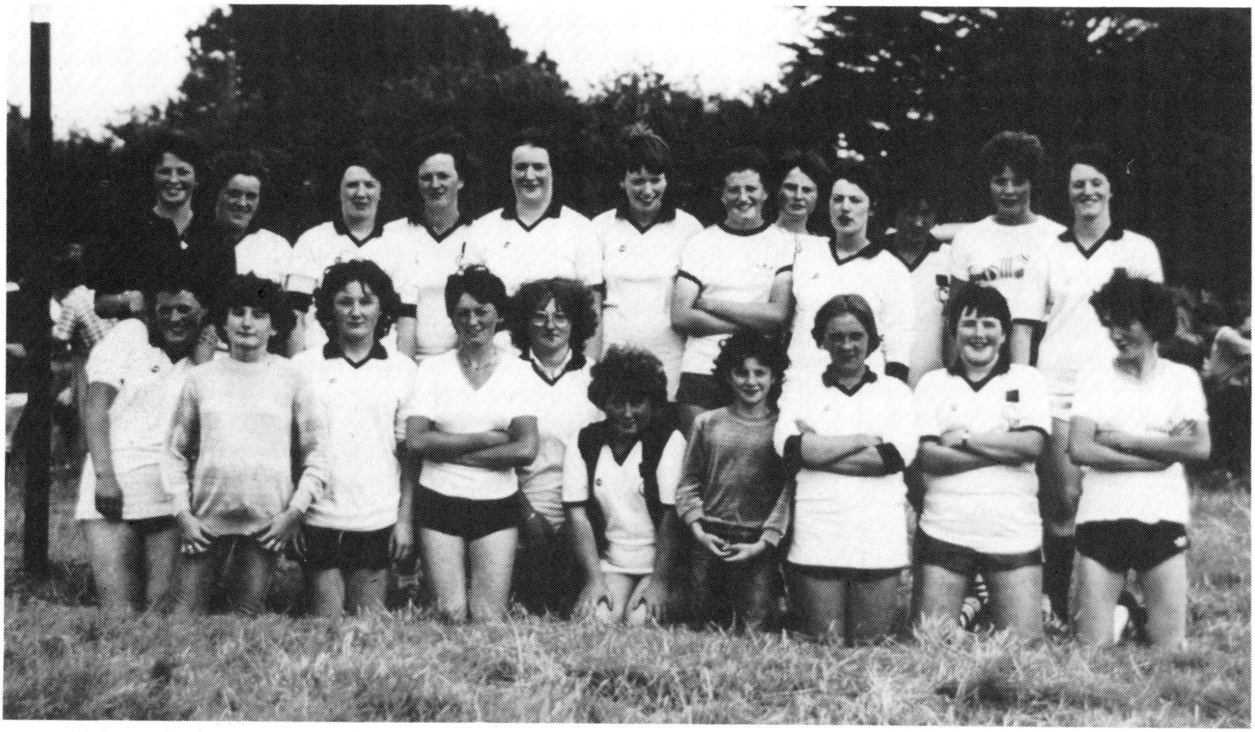

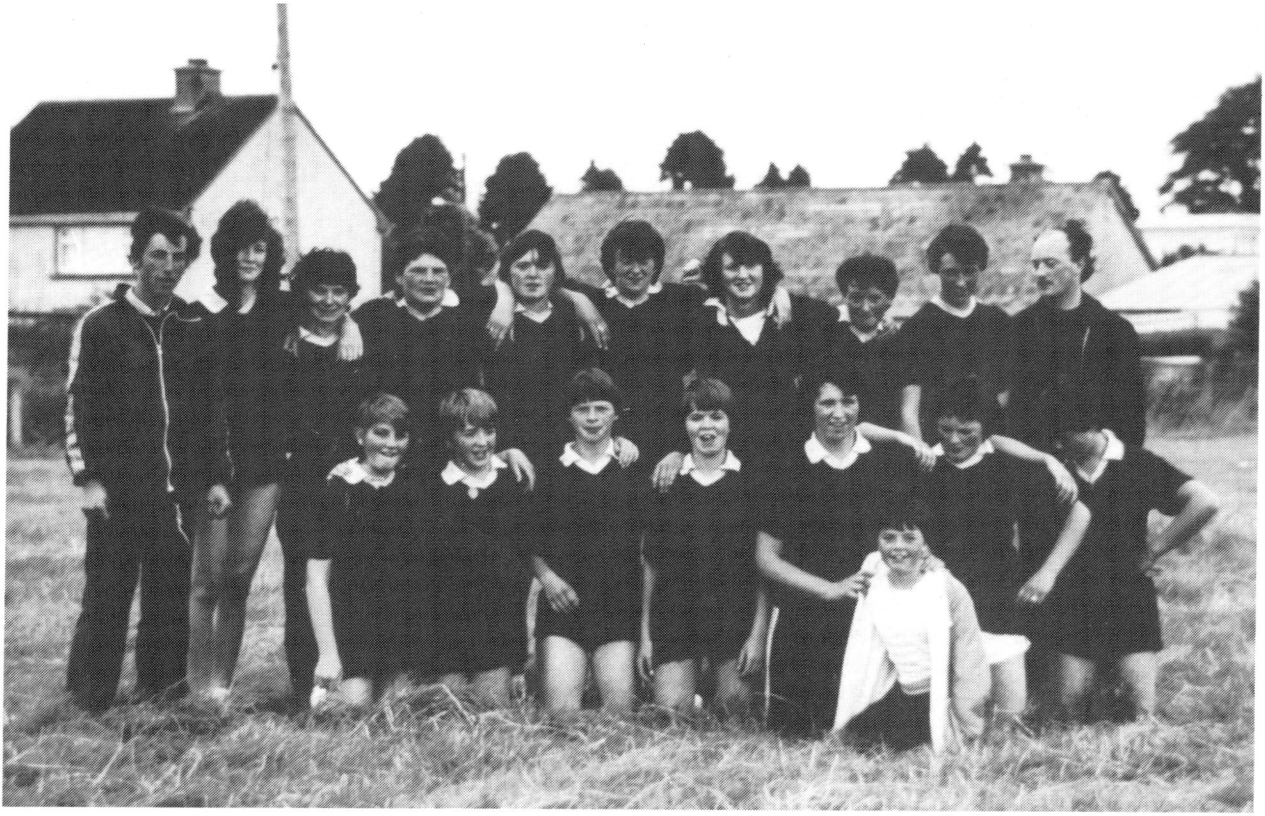

Two of the ladies football teams, and their mentors, who participated in the football blitz at the Rugby Club's Field Day.

77 Ardcroney (*opposite, above*) **Back** (l to r): Anne Coonan, Mary Kelly, Ellen Hill, Bernie Doheny, Colette Hogan, Margaret Cleary, Deirdre Cahalan, Anne Cleary, Nancy Hogan, Geraldine Cleary, Brigid Cleary, Ina Doheny. **Front:** Margaret Cahalan, Marie Cleary, Marguerite Cleary, Mary Coonan, Bridie Teefey (goalie), Michelle Tooher, Bernadette Cleary, Fiona Lewis, Madeline Cleary, Bernadette Darcy.
Like Shannon Rovers they discontinued playing football and most took up camogie.

78 Shannon Rovers (*opposite, below*) **Back** (l to r): Larry Dunne, Eileen O'Grady, Rosie Fox, Phil Fox, Sheila Dwyer, Mary Fox, Anne Burke (Kilbarron), Anne Burke (Springfield), Anne Hogan, Seamus Sullivan. **Front:** Siobhán O'Dwyer, Jeanette O'Meara, Eileen Hough, Brid O'Dwyer, Helen Fox, Kathleen Coen, Catherine O'Dwyer, Eileen O'Dwyer (child).
The football team was later dissolved and most took up camogie.

79 (*above*) Mary Coonan (Ardcroney) launches an attack.

80 Daly Family, 34 Castle/Pearse St c.1933. Back (l to r): Patrick, Richard (Rickie), Jack. **Middle:** May, Jonathan, Kathleen (née O'Halloran, Kerry), Kathleen (Kitty). **Front:** Dermot (a physician in Canada), Kevin.

Jonathan Daly had an undertaking, hackney and general merchant business where Cahill, Jeweller, now is. He also owned the yard in Bachelor's Walk/O'Rahilly St in which was located the original entrance to the gatehouse/baronial hall of Nenagh Castle.

81 (*above*) Claire and David Carmody, children of Precentor Dermot M. Carmody and Dr Maureen Carmody, Summerhill, later The Rectory, Church Rd. Claire (now Armit) works with Oxfordshire Social Services Child Protection Team. David is principal French horn player in the RTE Concert Orchestra.

82 (*below*) A group with more than a passing interest in the occasion – the first public performance of the re-organised Nenagh Brass Band in 1979. (l to r): Donal Morrissey, Benedine, with Brian in his arms; Murty and Tess Whelan, St Conlan's Rd; Phil and Eddie Sheridan, do., with son Terence (now organist, St. Mary's of the Rosary church). The location is Nolan's corner, Castle/Pearse St.

83 Three Generations of O'Donoghues, 14 Queen/Mitchel Street, c.1934. Back (l to r): Michael, Winifred, Ellen, and her husband James O'Brien, Limerick. **Middle:** Mrs Mary O'Donoghue, Josephine (Mrs John O'Gorman, Nenagh), Ciss (née Ryan), Mother Vincent (Order of Sacred Heart of Jesus and Mary). **Front:** Anthony O'Brien, Teresa O'Donoghue, Oliver O'Gorman, Florrie O'Donoghue, Moira O'Brien, Limerick.

84 (l to r): Gerard Irvine and his sister Maureen, St Patrick's Terrace, friends of Jack Ryan, the photographer, with Paddy and (front) Chrissy Ryan, Wolfe Tone Terrace, Jack's brother and sister.

… and neighbours as well, c.1951

85 Back (l to r): John Shalloe and Gerard Shalloe, Summerhill. **Middle:** Denis Butler, MacDonagh St; Paddy Shalloe, Summerhill; Matty O'Meara, MacDonagh St; Jimmy Butler, do; Michael Healy, do; Sean Whelan, Summerhill. **Front:** Jim Tierney, Rossa Place; Tom Ray, St. Joseph's Park; Michael O'Brien, MacDonagh St; Donal Whelan, Summerhill.

86 The wedding of Christopher Curtin & Kitty Slattery, Summer 1949

– Curtin (brother of groom); Mrs Curtin; Mrs Catherine Whelan (née Forde), Rossa Place; Nonie McGinn (née Whelan); Christy Curtin (groom), Limerick Junction & CIE, Nenagh; Sadie Whelan, Summerhill; Nonie Ryan, Castle/Pearse St; Kitty Slattery, Dublin Rd (bride); Christy (Sparks) Whelan, Rossa Place; Delia O'Connell (née Corbett), St Joseph's Park; Tony Whelan, Rossa Place; Elizabeth Corbett (née Forde); – Curtin (brother of groom; John Corbett; Nonie Slattery (née Forde), Dublin Rd; Peggy O'Meara, John's Lane; Betty Carroll (née Slattery), Borrisokane; Teresa O'Meara, John's Lane; Bernie Slattery, Knockanpierce; Paddy O'Brien, sacristan; Joan Curtin; – Curtin, father of the groom; Molly Healy, St. Joseph's Park.

87 The wedding of John McElwaine & Julia (Minnie) Dunne 28 Nov 1950.

Tommy Dunne, Cudville; – ; – ; Kitty Dunne, Ormond St; – ; – ; Gerard McAteer, Rathmullen, Co. Donegal; Paddy Brophy, Ormond St; Eamonn MacDaid, Rathmullen; Susan Flannery, Queen/Mitchel St; John McElwaine, Donegal, groom; Frank Flannery, Queen/Mitchel St; Julia (Minnie) Dunne, Ormond St, bride; Mary Brophy (née Maher), Ormond St; Nonie Ryan, Castle/Pearse St; Eileen Dunne; May McBride, Donegal; – ; Margaret (Mrs Gerard) Nolan, Barrack/Kenyon St; – ; Mary Dunne, Ormond St; Nell Hogan, Pound/Sarsfield St; – .

On Sunday 16 May 1982 a steam train, carriages packed with passengers, made a brief stop at Nenagh railway station. It was nineteen years since CIE/Córas Iompair Éireann had discontinued the use of steam traction, so the sight, sounds and smell were new experiences for the large crowd which thronged the station platform. [NY 139]

88, 89 (*above & below*) The crowded platform and a close-up of the crowd at the footbridge. The footbridge is now closed off as it is no longer needed since the second line of track was removed permanently.

90 (*above*) The full impact of the noise, particularly when the steam was emitted, wasn't music to a few pairs of younger ears!

91 For the steam train enthusiast the locomotive/engine is the main attraction. The two seen above are Locomotive No 171, built in 1913 for the Great Northern Railways, and Locomotive No 184, built in Inchicore in 1880 for Great Southern and Western Railways. The weekend was a busy one for the locomotives. Their grand tour included calls to Portarlington, Athlone, Athenry, and Limerick. They were on the way back to Dublin from Nenagh and thence to Belfast.

92 (*right*) Each engine had its own supply of coal; this was shovelled in almost constantly so that the steam pressure would be maintained.

93 Railway Station. (*opposite, above*) The locomotive/engine sheds, seen here in this 1980s picture, were demolished in the Spring of this year (1996). There have also been changes to the tracks. The track seen here in the foreground is still the upline to Dublin but the loop track to the right has been taken up. This loop track was to facilitate coinciding trains from opposite directions. Far left, barely discernible, is the cattle siding track; this too has gone. However, a new track is now in place just to the left of the main one and is used for shunting cement wagons.

94 A Dragon. (*opposite, below left*) This aluminium-painted cast iron figure was stolen from Nenagh railway embankment and recovered by Limerick Gardaí. It now graces Limerick railway station, erected there by Paddy Burns, formerly Nenagh. The dragon is a fabulous, supernatural monster of ancient and medieval mythologies, usually an embodiment of evil, and is commonly represented as a large winged lizard or fire-breathing serpent.

95 The water tower (*opposite, below right*), used to fill the boilers of the steam locomotives.

96 (*below*) Nenagh had a small complement of thatched houses up to the 1940s (at least), as seen in the aerial photograph presented by *The Irish Press* to Nenagh UDC [NY 54] and which now hangs in the Heritage Centre. This house, located in the Commonage (near the railway line), was photographed in the mid-1970s.

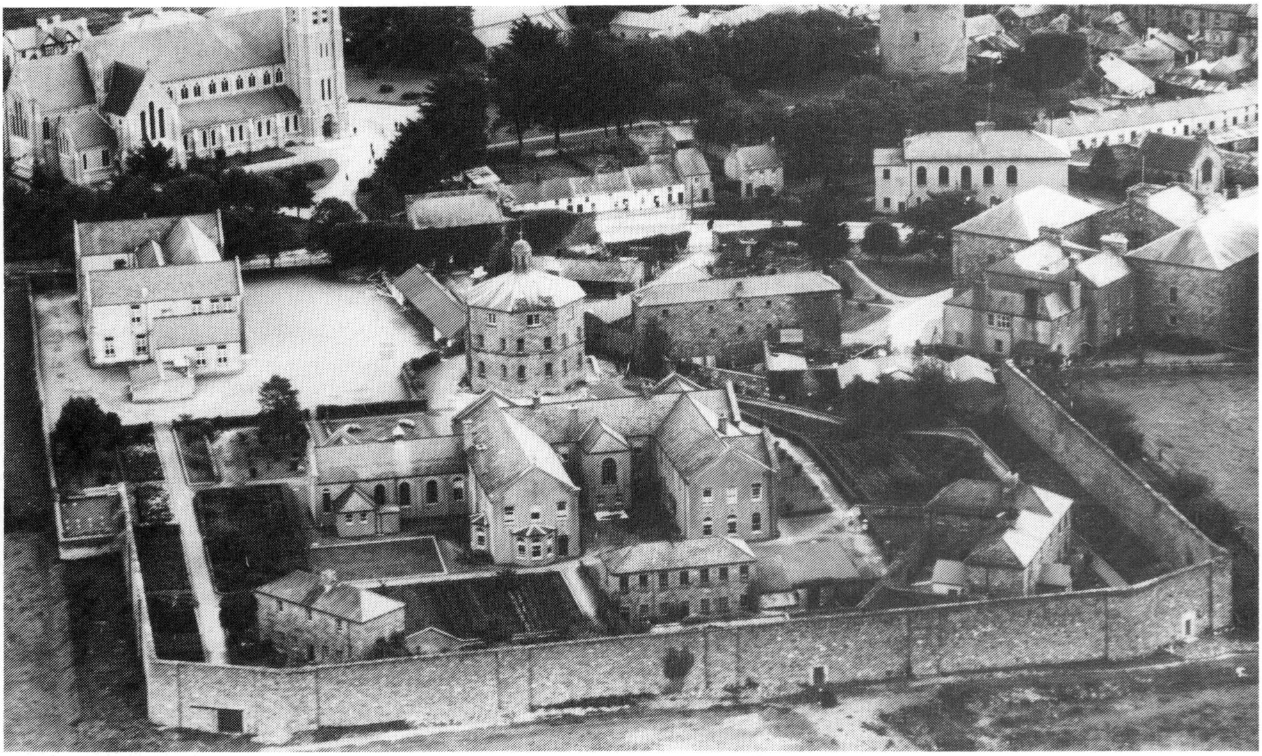

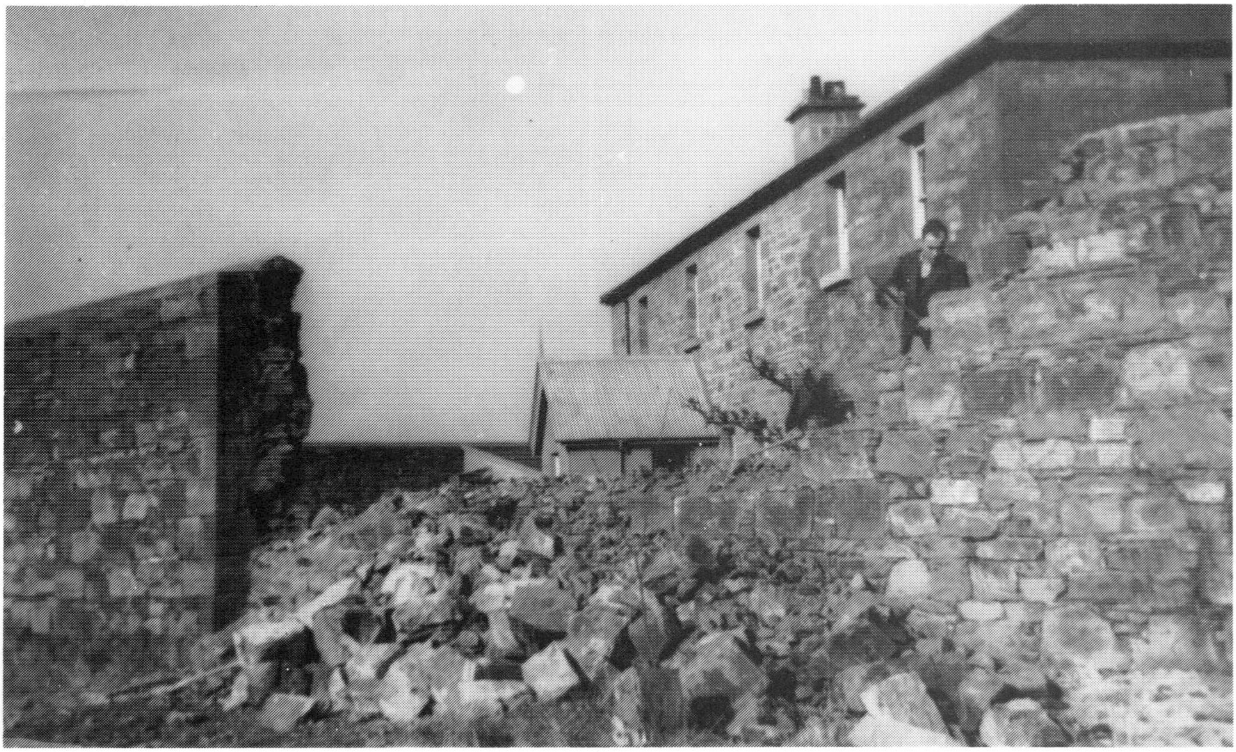

97 (*opposite, above*) This 1933 aerial view of Tipperary North Riding's former gaol/prison shows how much of the complex had survived since it ceased to be a gaol in 1886. In that year the local Community of the Sisters of Mercy acquired it for convent and school purposes. Note that most of the surrounding wall is still intact in 1933 – apart from the break to allow the Primary School (front, left) of 1911, and the Sisters graveyard of 1924, to extend into the adjoining field. On the far right a section of the perimeter wall has been relocated to let the surviving cell block into the yard of the courthouse. The convent (1913) occupies the site of the former women's prison. The three buildings between it and the rear perimeter wall are (l to r) the female infirmary, the laundry and the male infirmary. The former was utilised by the Sisters as a fee-paying school. The laundry was continued in use as such by the Sisters. The male infirmary became dormitories for the first boarders in 1929. Later it was assimilated into the secondary school for classrooms and a staff room. The gaol burial ground was in the space between the male infirmary and side perimeter wall.

98 (*opposite, below*) shows the early stages of the demolition of the perimeter wall between the male infirmary and the green field alongside, to make way for the first phase of the new St. Mary's Secondary School which opened in 1957.

After a further extension to the secondary school in1981 the former Governor's House was no longer needed for classrooms. The newly-founded Heritage Society obtained a lease on part of it to develop it as a heritage centre for Nenagh district. The Society sponsored an AnCO Community Youth Employment Scheme which undertook the restoration and decoration work, the building of display cases and adapting the rooms for exhibitions.

99 (*above*) The Foreman of the scheme was Tom Ryan, Birdhill, seen here on the front, left. The Trainees were **Back** (l to r): David Dooley, Borrisokane; Brendan Duignan, Dolla; Vivian Cahalan, Teryglass (painter). **Middle:** Martin Ryan, Toor, Newport (apprentice carpenter); Ger Shanahan, Toomevara (do.). **Front:** Laurence McGrath, Newport (do); Kevin Gleeson, Nenagh.

100 (*above*) **The Official Opening of Nenagh District Heritage Centre,** Friday 17 May 1985: The blessing by Most Rev. Michael A. Harty, Bishop of Killaloe (left) and Right Rev. Walton Empey, Bishop of Limerick and Killaloe, now Archbishop of Dublin. **Front** (l to r): Dan Mullane, Acting Hon Secretary, NDHS; Eamonn De Stafort, Shannonside Tourism; Very Rev. Joseph O'Brien, P.P., Bourney, Curator, Toomevara Folk Museum; Very Rev. Edward Whyte, P.P., Cloughjordan, Committee, NDHS; Mary Grace, Vice-Chairman and Trustee, NDHS; (behind her) Patrick Ryan, MCC, Limerick, Director Shannonside Tourism; Stiophán Ó Flannabhra, Patron. **Back row** includes (l to r): founders Neil Corrigan (with beard), Ger Lewis, James Gleeson, Peter Hogan, (to his right) Tim Maher, Patron. **Middle** includes (r to l): (in front of N Corrigan) Archdeacon Eric Stanley, Michael Joy, Patron, Luke Murtagh, C.E.O., TNR V.E.C.; David Slattery, senior architect, OPW; Martin Maher, Co. Librarian.

101 (*opposite, above*) (l to r): Tony Brazil, Chairman Shannonside Tourism; Sean Browne, Manager, Regions/Environment Bord Fáilte; Noel Clifford, Chairman, Nenagh UDC; John Ryan, TD, Leas Cheann Comhairle, who spoke on behalf of Mr Michael Moynihan, TD, Minister for Tourism (who had been ill that morning) at the reception afterwards in the Convent primary school auditorium; Frank Lewis, Chairman TNR Co. Council and first Chairman of NDHS who cut the tape, deputising for the Minister; Donal Murphy, Chairman, NDHS; Michael O'Kennedy, TD; Terry McCarthy, Regional Manager, AnCO.

102 (*opposite, below*) **The Schoolroom** became the most popular exhibition jointly with The Shop, both recreated in 1940s-1950s mode. Behind the master's desk (formerly in Latteragh N.S.) Liam O'Byrne, N.T., has his Puckane class do a quiz, monitored also by John O'Grady, graphic artist and AnCO trainee.

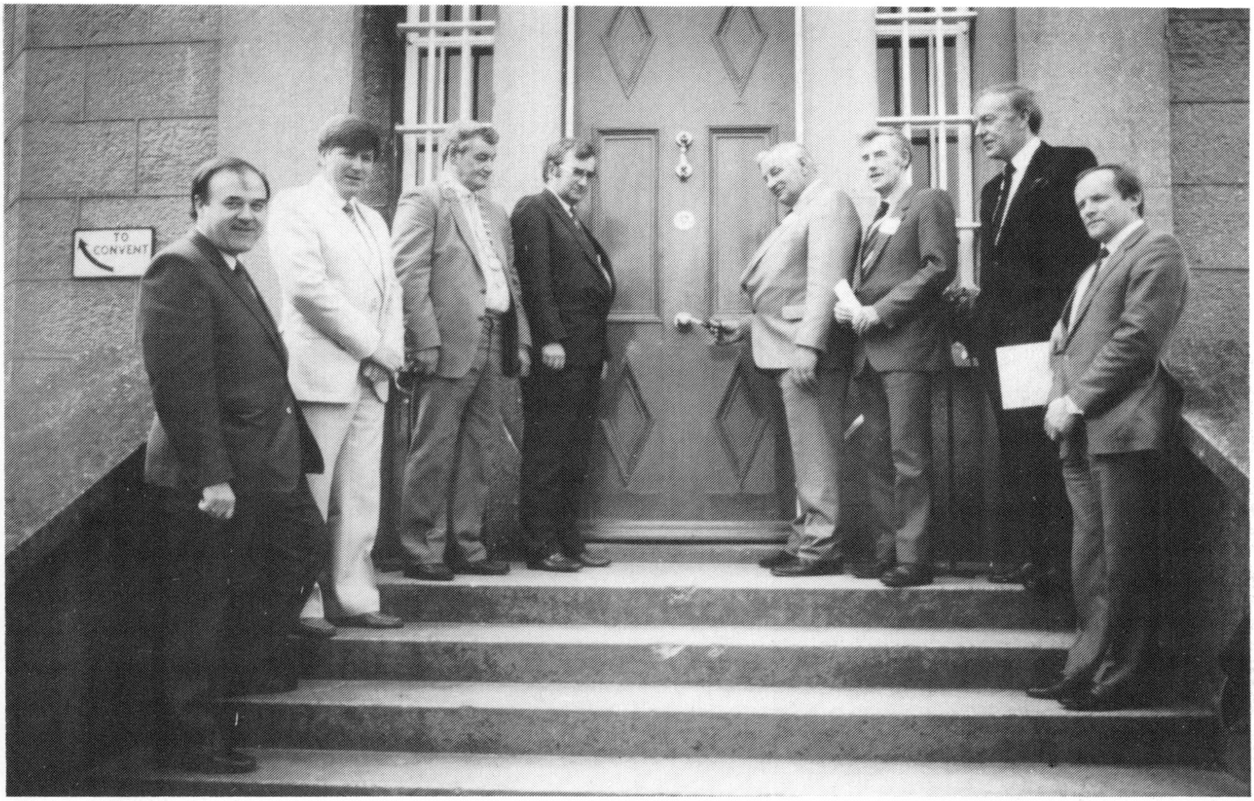
TO
CONVENT

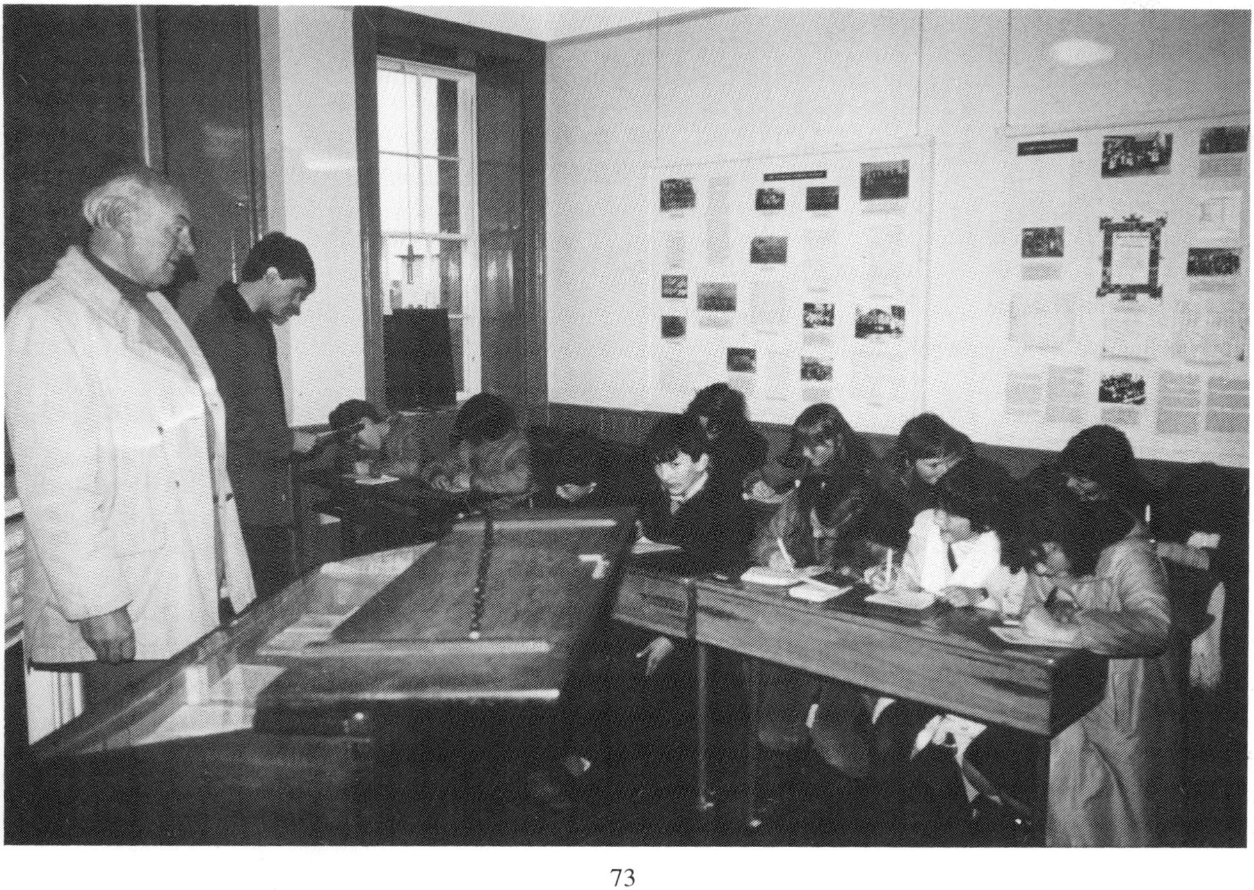

103 The Gatehouse facade caused Nenagh District Heritage Society, formed 22 April 1982, considerable work and expenditure – one-third of the total £96,000 spent on renovation of the two premises, apart from the AnCO payments to its workforce over two years. Pictured here during the course of the repairs to the stonework are Jim Kemmy,TD, master stonemason; Neil Corrigan, architect; David Slattery, OPW, all voluntary consultants; John Cotter of Top Quarries, contractors; Sr Kathleen Minogue, Trustee; Donal Murphy, Trustee.

104 (*below*) The AnCO reconstruction team in the Gatehouse reception room. It is now the family history research centre's reception area. Note the narrow stairs leading to the condemned cells and scaffold site. **Back** (l to r): Timmy Hourigan, Lissenhall; Paddy Ryan, Birdhill; P. J. Ryan, do.; Seán Mulcahy, Ballywilliam; Dermot Donovan, Ballina (on stairs); Noel McCarthy, Killaloe; Liam Woulfe, Limerick; Gerry Keays, Ballywilliam; Tom Ryan (Foreman), Birdhill; Francis Healy, Ballywilliam. **Front:** Pat Daly, Ballina; –.

74

105 BEFORE and **106 AFTER** – one of the two exercise yards for prisoners condemned to death by hanging and confined to the Gatehouse. The yard had accumulated ninety-eight years of debris. It became the office for Eamonn De Stafort (at desk), Environmental Officer, Shannonside Tourism, whose Tourist Information Office was out front in one of the prisoners' and turnkeys' (warders) day-rooms, all now part of Tipperary North Family History Foundation's research centre suite. (l to r): Brendan Russell, Regional Tourism Manager; Niall Reddy, Executive Director-Development Bord Fáilte; Frank Lewis, Chairman, Shannonside Tourism.

107 Planting Trees on the Green, St. Flannan's Street, 1950. (*above*) Pupils of St Mary's Boys national school and the Christian Brothers primary school. The adults are (l to r): Bro. Craven, CBS; Eddie Bourke, N.T.; Pat Harrold, Horticultural Advisor; Joe Daly, N.T.; Tomás Cleary, N.T.; Dan O'Keeffe, UDC.

108 The St Patrick's Day Parade was revived in 1979 and made an immediate impact with participants and viewers. (*opposite, above*): Paddy Richardson, Chairman, formally opens the 1983 parade. (l to r): Tony McCormack, Town Clerk; Rev. John O'Driscoll, C.C.; John McGinley, Co. Manager and Commandant, FCA; Joseph O'Connor, UDC, Chairman, Nenagh Town Traders; Billy Bailey, Chairman, Nenagh UDC; Geraldine McNulty, Secretary, Parade Committee; Noel Ryan, Chairman, Nenagh Chamber of Commerce; John Ryan, TD, Leas Cheann Comhairle; Superintendent Peter Smith; (below platform) Ned Spillane, steward. The other Committee members were: Michael McNulty, vice-Chairman & PRO; Michelle Spearman, Asst Hon Sec; Denis O'Sullivan, Hon Treasurer; Billy Barry, Asst Hon Treasurer; Denis Ryan, Chief Steward, Stiophán Ó Flannabhra, Michael Boland, Jimmy Moran, Jimmy Bourke, Thomas Feighery, Johnny McLoughlin, Tony Langton.

109 Community Radio 1980. (*opposite, below*) Long before local radio stations were introduced, RTE visited communities and serviced a week of radio produced by locals. The RTE van parked beside the Christ the King statue, formerly Jamsey The Monument, and opposite Kilroy's furniture stores, formerly the Rialto cinema and now Sheahan's hardware suppliers. On the final day (l to r): Noel Shoer, – of RTE, Nancy Murphy, Donal Murphy, Paddy Richardson, Padraig O'Neill, the RTE producer, Noel Ryan, Liam O'Byrne, Joseph O'Connor, and (seated) Austin Dolan.

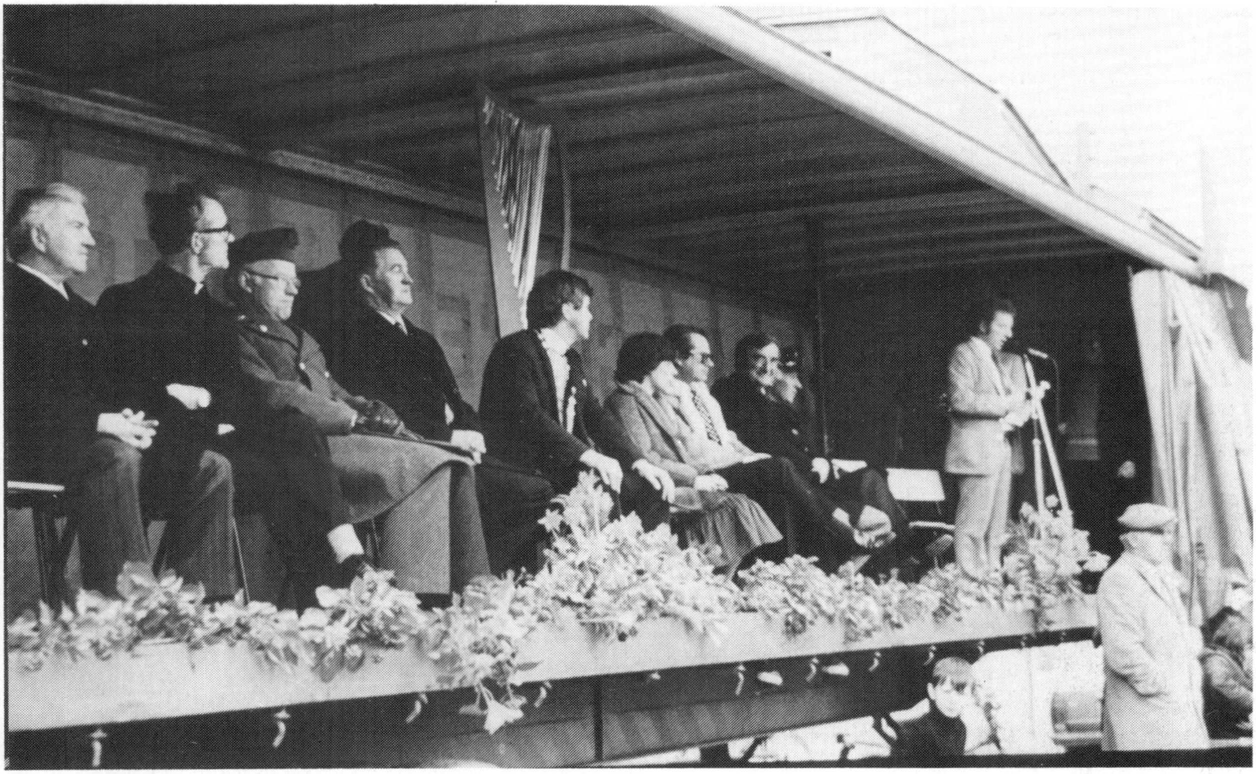

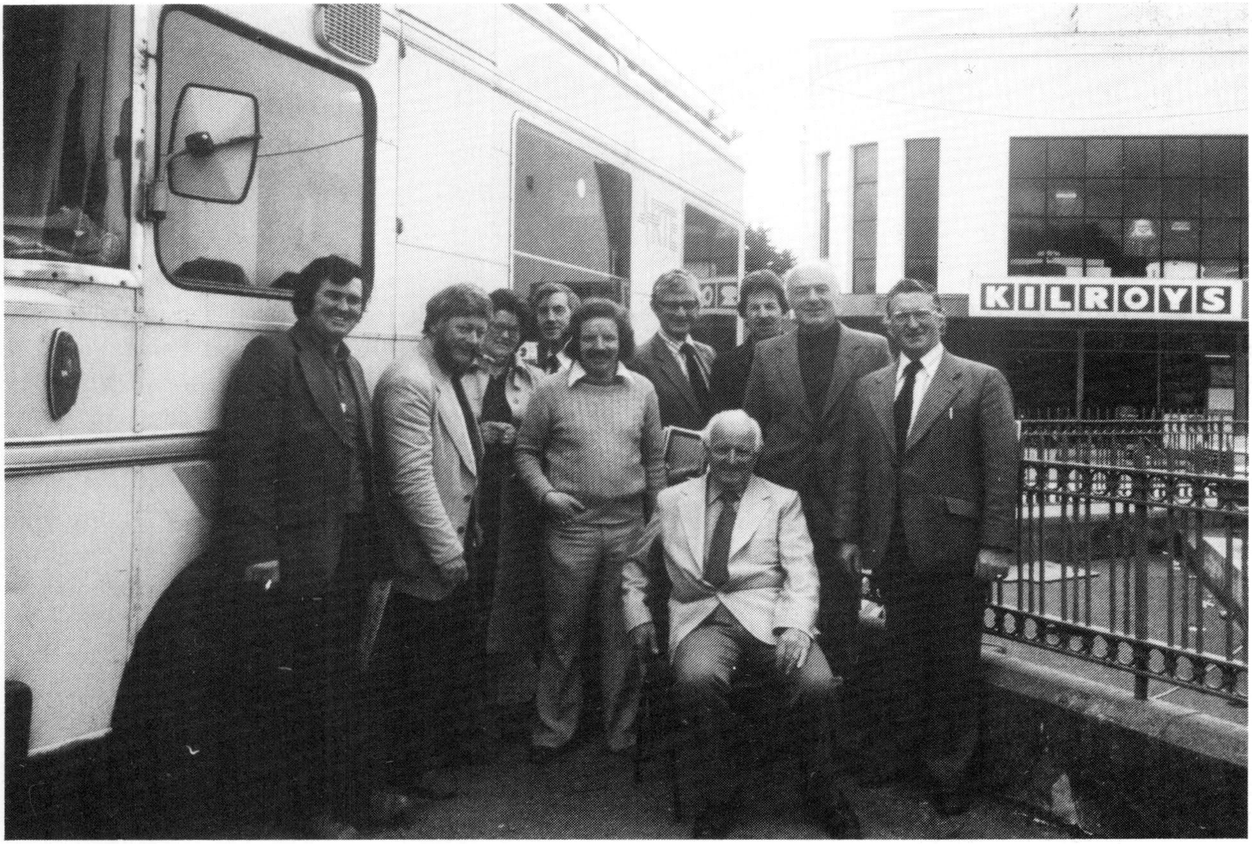
KILROYS

110 The First Nenagh Chamber of Commerce, founded Dec 1956. **Back** (l to r): Michael Hackett, victualler, 94 Silver St; Christy Lally, Ivy Cleaners, Summerhill; Joe Bergin, grocer, 90 Silver St; Tom Ferris, grocer, 1 Mitchel St whose wife Thérèse ran Power's pharmacy, 62 Pearse St; John Healy, CIE Stationmaster; Tony Healy, victualler, 32 Pearse St; Dick Bourke, draper, 81 Pearse St; **Middle**: Paddy Walsh, wholesale merchant (leather, paper etc), 2 Mitchel St; Tony Scroope, grocer, 60 Pearse St; Eddie John McGrath, vintner, 56 Pearse St; Paddy Tobin, jeweller, 55 Pearse St; John De Loughrey, pharmacist, 15 Pearse St; Ned McQuaid, Central Hotel, 17-18 Kenyon St; Paddy Cadell, Hibernian Hotel, 23 Pearse St; **Front**: Tony Boland, UDC, painting contractor, 8 Wolfe Tone Tce; Tom White, Secretary, Irish Aluminium Co. (even then advertising under the heading 'Castle Brand'); P.J. McDwyer, general secretary of the National Council of Chambers of Commerce; Joe Bergin, President, wholesale merchant (confectionery etc), Cudville; Seamus Cleary, Secretary, draper, 57 Pearse St; Frank Cassidy, motor factor & garage, 16 Pearse St; Kevin O'C Bernal, UDC, farmer & milk vendor, Brookwatson. Approaching the Chamber's fortieth birthday, just three of the twenty founders, Messrs Hackett, T. Healy and Walsh, are still in the same businesses, among the seven founders still alive.

Walkabout Nenagh (Relay Books, 1994) treats of many of the above personalities and of the occupiers before and after of their premises: 'thrusting enterprise and solid public service by natives and blow-ins alike; cultural success, sporting prowess and voluntary dedication to community development and welfare'.

111 This Castle/Pearse Street postcard was commissioned by Harris Newsagent at No. 76. The Shell petrol sign is outside Moloney's garage, now Ger Gavin's Pound Shop. The chairs and table are outside Robinson's drapery and hardware, now Dunne's Stores. O'Shea's newsgency is at No. 73. They moved to No. 76 in 1971 when proprietors Mrs Evelyn and Olive Harris retired from business. There are Morris Minor and Ford Anglia cars a-plenty. Double and skew-ways parking was popular even then!

112 D. Herriott, Chemist, 9 Castle/Pearse St. In the doorway is Mrs Mary Herriott. It is said she was in San Francisco during the 1906 earthquake. Her son Dave and his wife Nellie (née O'Leary) carried on the business until the 1980s. It continues as a pharmacy under the proprietorship of Catherine Harnett.

113 *The Vagabond King*. (l to r): Matt Manley (Casin Cholet), Paddy McLoughlin (the hangman), Jimmy Spearman (chorus), Frankie Sherlock (Toison d'Or), Joe Daly (the Captain). The fight scenes were brilliantly arranged by Joe also.

The lead roles were played by Ena Harold, Dublin, and Gus Barrett, Shannon. It was produced by Londoner Douglas Neill and cost a record £5,000. *The Vagabond King* is a light opera set in the Paris of Louis XI whose part was played by John Riggs-Miller. The *Guardian* described it as a wonderful mix of music and drama, best described as a musical play. Over 100 people in all were involved in the production from behind the scenes to standing in front of the spotlights. Tommy Kennedy was stage manager. The musical ran from Sun 23 March to Sun 30 March 1980 inclusive.

114 (l to r): Gerry Scanlon (Oliver le Dain), Marie Hassett (née Bergin) (Lady Mary) and Seamus McCarthy. Both Gerry and Seamus brought great laughs from the audience despite the fact that there was very little comedy script in the production.

115 (*left*) ***The Hasty Heart*** had a Far East war hospital setting for the Nenagh Players. The reality was a draughty Town Hall in a freezing March 1958 – John De Loughrey had a hot water bottle in the bed in the tropical setting. **Back** (l to r): Bill O'Leary, David Hodgins, Seamus Cleary. **Front:** Jimmy Hayes, Fergus Considine, John De Loughrey, John Riggs-Miller, Olive Harris, Mike Keller. Another John Patrick play, *The Curious Savage*, celebrated the Players' golden jubilee in Nov 1993 – and 1943 founder Olive Harris played the lead.

116 (*right*) ***Arsenic and Old Lace***, 'a classical black comedy', 'induces a state of comic euphoria', by Joseph Kesserling, was first produced in New York, 1941, London, 1942, Nenagh Players, 1955, revived for the Dublin Theatre Festival 1985 and the Nenagh Players 5-10 November 1985 as their 68th production and opening their 43rd season. The Brewster sisters (Harris & Quigley) have a mission, to bring relief to elderly, lonely gentlemen – terminal relief,

considerably administered in elderberry wine. Their twelfth corpse and a criminal nephew's (Tobin) twelfth corpse, which arrives in the boot of his car, cause confusion, particularly for another crazy nephew (Riggs-Miller) who digs the cellar graves, believing he is the USA President extending the Panama Canal. **Back** (l to r): Kevin Walshe; Dick Tobin (also 1955 cast), Tom Hayes; Rose Shaw (now Cleary) (prompts); Bryan Geaney; Noel Ryan (Director) – his ninth with the Players – his previous included two Brian Friels, two Agatha Christies, an O'Casey and *The Man Who Came to Dinner*; Kevin McLoughlin, who had experience with the Lyric, Belfast; Metro, Dublin; The Runners, Tullamore; Sheila Geaney (née Finn). **Middle:** John De Loughrey (also 1955 cast); Seamus McCarthy, John Riggs-Miller, a 1943 founder (also 1955 cast), one-time rep player with Ronald Ibbs and Anew McMaster, Best Supporting Actor, Charleville Festival, 1981. **Front:** Olive Harris, founder (also 1955 cast), gold medallist Féile Luimní, 1947; Oliver Healy, a founder, playing since 1939 (Nenagh Dramatic Class) (also 1955 cast); Mary McGrath (née Cleary); Doley Quigley, nominated for Best Supporting Actress, Scariff 1981. **Not in picture:** Tommy Kennedy, stage manager, winner of award at Scariff Festival, 1981; Liam Gleeson.

117 This photograph c.1965 sums up the camaraderie engendered by sport: county, national, and international champions, some with second sporting affiliations, at a light-hearted training session in the old Showgrounds. John Lawlor, a Dubliner and geologist at the Mogul mines at Silvermines, seen here swinging a hammer, was placed fourth in the Olympic Games at Rome in 1960. **Behind** (l to r): Billy Gaffney, a CIE employee from Goulds Cross, a former cyclist and cross-country runner who learned pole vaulting in the adjoining Horticultural Hall, reached twelve feet and a national silver medal, later took up pitch-and-putt; Tom Holmes, a County Council clerk, former soccer player and referee, middle distance and marathon runner, who held all officerships in Nenagh Olympic AC at various times; Edward Ryan, a student from Kenyon St, now a doctor in Canada, one of the four athletes who won the O'Dwyer cup for the county juvenile team championship in 1964 and 1965; Liam Gleeson, a clerk from Ballintotty who later set up his own accountancy practice, Gaffney's tutor and who himself rose the national pole vault record in nine steps over twelve seasons, 1961-72, won ten national pole vault and two javelin titles and made Nenagh an athletic household name in the Sixties; Michael McGrath, an Irish Aluminium Company employee, a member of the only Nenagh team to win both county novice and junior cross-country titles, simultaneously playing rugby with Nenagh Ormond and their Captain in 1974, father of Jim, a recent NORFC stalwart.

118 (*above*) **Fisherfolk at the Nenagh River, 1965. Back** (l to r): Jack Kelly, Ormond Street; Michael O'Brien, St. Joseph's Park; Martin O'Brien, do. **Front:** Joe Mitchell, do; Denis (Din) O'Brien, do.

119 (*left*) Din O'Brien, holding a 5 1/2 lb trout, caught in the Nenagh River on the same day as above.

120 Brian Tansey's departure in October 1963 to take up duty as Chief Asst Co. Engineer, Cavan, marked by a staff group at the Courthouse, Nenagh. **Back** (l to r): John C. Finn, Chief Asst Co. Engineer (Roads), later Deputy Chief Engineer, Dublin Co. Council; Jimmy Leahy, Clerk, Engineer's Dept.; Breandán S. Ó Foighil, Asst Co. Engineer, Roscrea, later Head of Engineering, Regional Technical College, Galway, later Technical Services Officer, North-Eastern Health Board; Patrick J. Pearse, Asst Co. Engineer, Nenagh-Newport area; Michael Kerrane, Asst Co. Engineer, Thurles area; Donal Murphy, C.O., Accounts, later Personnel Officer, Mid-Western Health Board; Joe Murphy, C.O., Motor Taxation, later S.E.O., Dublin Co. Council; Jerry Quinlan, C.O., Housing, later practising Chartered Accountant, Nenagh; Kevin Hayes, Chief Asst Co. Engineer, Housing, later Senior Executive Engineer, Galway; Roger Corcoran, Asst Co. Engineer, Borrisokane area; Tom Holmes, C.O., Engineer's Dept., later Staff Officer, Computer Section; Seán Murphy, Chief Asst Co. Engineer, Planning, later Limerick County Manager. **4th Row:** Michael O'Connell, C.O., Housing, later Contracts Controller, National Building Agency; John O'Donoghue, Storekeeper; John Mounsey, Asst Storekeeper; John Houlihan, Staff Officer, Rates; T. P. Sheehan, C.O., Accounts, later S.E.O., Dublin Co. Council, Michael O'Brien, Senior Draughtsman. **3rd Row:** Ann McDonnell, Co. Manager's Secretary; Elizabeth Smee, C.T., General Purposes, later Moloney, Holycross; Nora Cummins, C.T., Engineer's Dept., later Quigley, Killoscully; Billy Allen, Staff Officer, General Purposes, later Town Clerk, Clonmel; Ina Gleeson, Public Health Nurse; Agnes Lynch, C.T., Accounts, later Toohey, Dunkerrin; Mary Maher, C.T., Accounts, later Barry, Wexford; Tom Kirwan, Staff Officer, Accounts, later Finance Officer. **2nd Row:** Maura Purcell, C.T., Co. Hospital, later Molumby, Thurles; Seamus Ó Domhnaill, County Surgeon; Anna Reddan, C.T., Accounts, later Browne, Cork; Peggy Roche, C.T., Housing, now TNR Co. Enterprise Officer; Cathal MacArtain, County Accountant, later Regional Manager, IDA, Dundalk; Thérèse Butler, C.T., General Purposes, later MacDomhnaill. **Front:** John M. Murray, County Engineer; Sean T. O'Neill, Town Clerk; Brian Tansey, Housing Engineer; John P. Flynn, County Manager; Thomas Brophy, County Secretary; Dr. Patrick B O'Meara, County Medical Officer; John P. McCarthy, Chief Fire Officer.

Upward and frequently outward mobility has been a feature of local government staff life; see *The Two Tipperarys*, pp 207-210.

121 (*right*) **Outing to Tramore,** c.1955, by 'the Courthouse crowd' and friends. **Back** (l to r): – , Teresa Newman, later Dempsey, – , Dessie Finn, St. Joseph's Park, – . **Front:** Frank Manley, Wolfe Tone Terrace; Michael Darcy, Thurles; Ivy Ryan, Parteen, later Darcy; (in front of her) Chris Cahill, Ennis; (also seated) Pat Troy, Drom; Phil Murphy, Sarsfield Street; Maureen McCormack, Glenakilty, later Kelly; Anne Barrett, Summerhill, later Barry.

122 (*below*) **Openness, Transparency, and Count Ability,** for the Borrisokane area, TNR Co. Council election tallies, 1985. **Count staff:** John O'Donoghue (standing), Nora Quigley (née Cleary), Joan Glennon (née Neville), Tony Forde, John Deely, Peter Hogan (back to camera). The amicable coalition of interested parties include: **Back** (l to r): Tim Liffey, Billy Foley, Ger Darcy, Denis Darcy, Noel Brennan, Pat Hough; **Middle:** Jim Darcy (left), Michael Hough (2nd from right). **Front:** Bridie Lewis (née Ryan), Mary (Birdy) McGrath (née Meagher), Tom Keogh, Johnny McGrath.

The first count; Jim Casey, FF, 1,089; Michael Hough, FF, 966; Tony McKenna, 876; Liam Whyte, FG, 742; John Carroll, FF, 616; Paddy Brennan, FG, 518; Ger Darcy, FG, 461; Jim Hough, Lab, 288; Maureen Carmody, Lab 277.

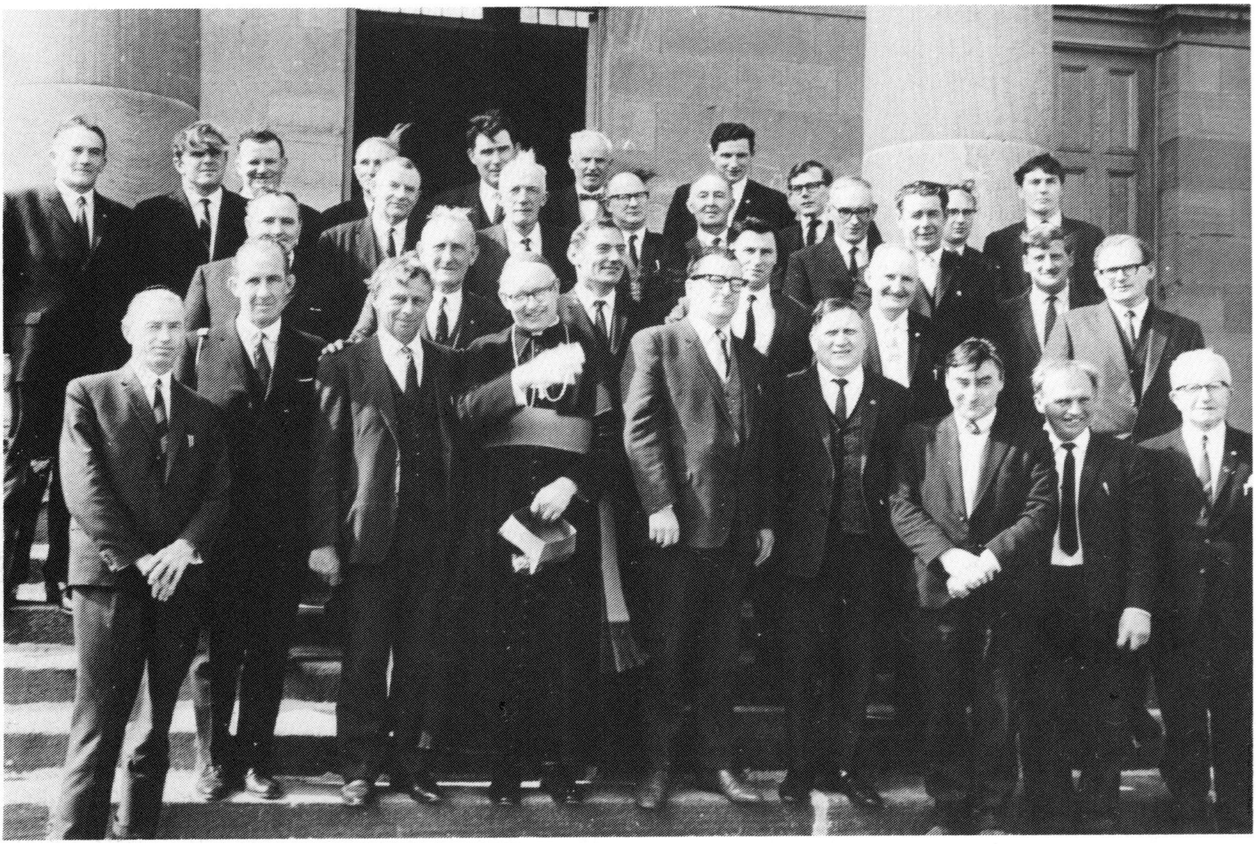

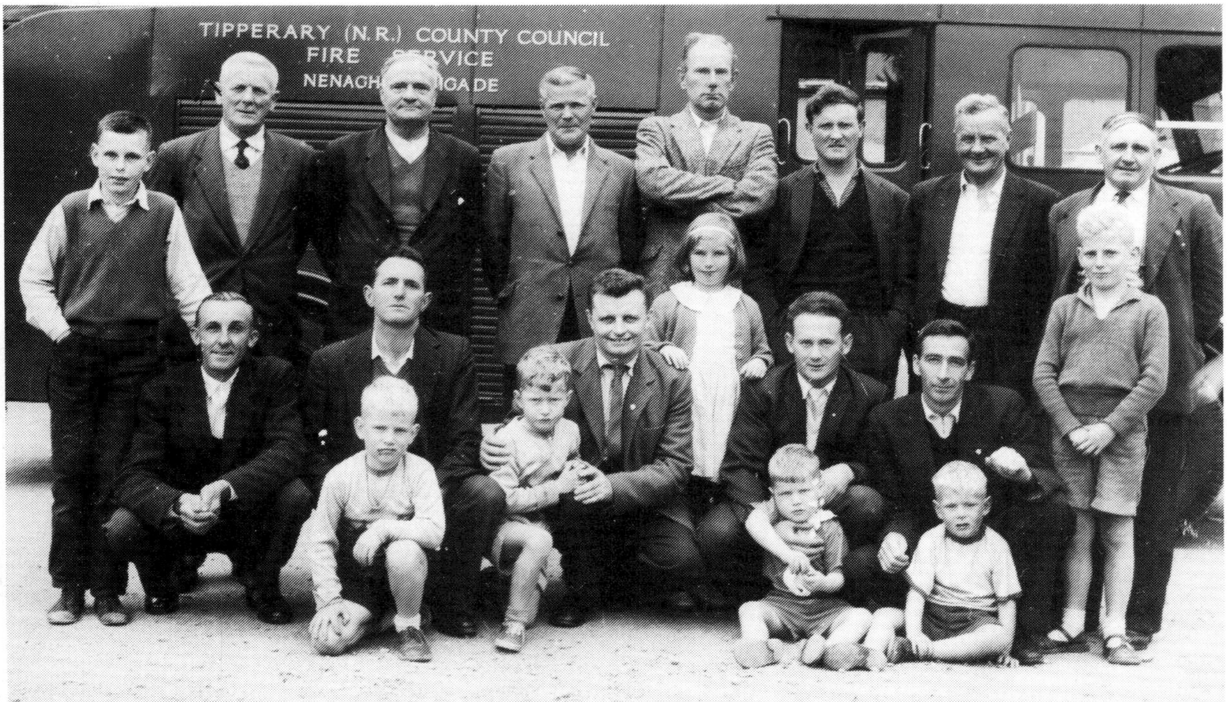
TIPPERARY (N.R.) COUNTY COUNCIL
FIRE

123 (*opposite, above*) **New Council Greets New Bishop:** A visit in early 1968 to TNR County Council, elected in 1967, by Dr Michael A. Harty, Bishop of Killaloe, consecrated in 1967. **Back** (l to r): Joe Bergin, Nenagh; John Doyle, Holycross; Jim Mounsey, Clashnevin, Nenagh; John Cahalan, Borrisokane; Jim Darcy, Ardcroney; Bob Stakelum, Thurles staff; Michael Smith, Behagloss, Roscrea, later TD, Senator, and Minister; Willie Moloney, Nenagh staff, now Clare County Manager; Tom Holmes, Nenagh staff; Noel Cleary, Nenagh staff. **3rd Row:** Jack Murphy, Thurles; Dan Moylan, Rathnaleen, Nenagh; Billy Allen, Nenagh staff; Martin Brislane, Coologue, Toomevara; Tom Kirwan, Acting Co. Secretary. **2nd Row:** John Finn, Chief Asst Co. Eng.; John Fanning, TD, Two-Mile-Borris; Ned Kennedy, Templetuohy; Edw. Meagher, Templemore; Martin Cosgrave, Longford, Templemore; John Houlihan, Acting Co. Accountant; Dan Kennedy, Rearcross; Michael O'Connell, Nenagh staff. **Front:** Tom Brophy, Acting Asst. Co. Mgr; Jack Murray, Co. Engineer; Liam Whyte, later Senator, Aglish, Borrisokane; Dr. Harty; John Ryan, Nenagh, later TD; Tom Shanahan, Roscrea; Tom Dunne, TD, Thurles; Tom Moloney, Holycross; Pádraig de Buitléir, Co. Manager. **Absent:** Paddy Tierney, TD, Coolbawn; Paddy Ryan (Philips), Templederry.

It was this Council which unanimously agreed to separate Managers for North and South Ridings. T. Brophy became the NR's third Manager in Feb 1970 – see *The Two Tipperarys*, Epilogue and Appendix Nine.

124 (*opposite, below*) **The Nenagh Fire Brigade,** c.1960. **Back** (l to r): Michael Ryan, Jun.; Mick Ryan (Cap), Knockanpierce; Dinny O'Meara, Wolfe Tone Tce; Tommy Dunne, Cudville, Station Officer; Willie Ryan, Summerhill, Sub-Station Officer; Danny Hassett, Tyone; Jack Nagle, Clare St; Tommy Meagher, Ormond St. **Front:** Paddy McCarthy, William St; Eddie Griffin, do; Sean Mounsey, St. Flannan St; Paddy O'Meara, Gortlandroe; Johnny McGrath, Silver St; the Ryan Brigade, Willie's children: Jim, Tony, Marion, Martin, Rody, and Hugh. All were local authority staff, except builder W. Ryan.

125 (*above*) **The Changing of the Guards,** January 1986. (l to r): Chris Middleton & son Cathal, Seán English, Bríd Ryan (Dept. of Justice), Frank Hynes, Detective Cecil Gleeson, Billy Kelly, Inspector Pat Moriarty, Sergeant Pat Walsh, Donal Ryan, Pat Fox, Martin Delaney, Eddie Scanlon, Gemma Cullen. The door is closed before the transfer to Banba Square. [NY 32,158: see the Barracks story and drawing, *Walkabout Nenagh*, pp 63-4.]

Locurdes 1960

939

126 Killaloe Diocesan pilgrimage to Lourdes, 1960. Some of the participants went by air from Shannon Airport, others travelled over land via Holyhead, Dover, Calais and Paris. The photograph was taken after Most Rev. Joseph Rodgers, Bishop of Killaloe, had led the ceremony for the blessing of the sick. The backdrop to the picture is the splendid basilica. Throughout their stay in Lourdes the invalids are looked after by medical and nursing staff who travel with them from the diocese. Meals are prepared for them in the ward kitchen.

Rev. M. Queally, Adm, Ennis; Nurses –; Cantwell, Nancy Tynan, Maureen Moroney, Nenagh hospital; Rev. Kieran O'Gorman (behind N. Tynan); Ciss O'Donoghue, Ballingarry (beside M. Moroney), In the front row behind the three stretchers are (l to r): Séamus Ó Domhnaill, County Surgeon, Nenagh; –; – Coughlan, Matron, Ennis, who was in charge of nursing and catering; Most Rev. Joseph Rodgers; Rev. - O'Donoghue; Dr Eileen O'Donnell, Nenagh. Very Rev. Edmund Murphy, P.P., Silvermines, an organiser (extreme right).

127 (*above*) **Ready to Shoot?** Bishop Joseph Rodgers is consulted by film cameraman Jim Doyle before inspecting the F(orsa) C(ósanta) Á(itiúla) guard of honour. The Bishop, accompanied by Rev. Edmund Murphy, Administrator during the final years of Archdeacon Stephen Slattery's tenure as Parish Priest, has come from the P.P.'s house out of picture to the right. The FCA party includes Michael Hegarty, MacDonagh St (3rd from left) and Willie O'Donoghue, St. John's Tce (4th).

128 (*left*) **The Sign of the Cross.** The old cross was removed from the spire of St. Mary's of the Rosary in December 1959. Canon Michael Hamilton, P.P., Nenagh, is seen here blessing a new, less ornate, one prior to its elevation. He had initiated major improvements in St. Mary's of the Rosary church in 1956 (see *St. Mary's of the Rosary, Nenagh, 1896-1990*, ed Rev. Pat Cotter).[NY 71-3]

129 (*above*) **St. John's Well** 'is signposted down a pathway beside the Nenagh River, to the right just short of the [Scott's] bridge. Here, in the name of St. John, the pagan rites of Mid-Summer's Eve (24 June) became subsumed into a Christian pilgrimage on that day which continues as an annual parish Mass' – *A trip through Tipperary Lakeside* (RELAY Books, 1997). Canon (later Monsignor) Michael Hamilton is about to start the proceedings at the re-opening in 1959 following extensive refurbishments of the site by a working party which he led and which included Martin O'Connor, at extreme left of picture 130 right.

130 (*right*) **Also present:** John McGrath, Co. Secretary, – , Kathleen Ryan, St. Joseph's Park; Ann Creagh, do.; – ; – ; (front) Joan Creagh, do.

131 (*above*) **Nenagh Girls School,** pre-1914. This is one of the earliest photographs of a group of Nenagh schoolgirls to surface to date. The location is probably a classroom in the new (1911) primary school. The names supplied with the photograph relate to rows down by the wall, not by the desk. However, while there are nine names given for the back row (i.e. by the wall on the right) only seven children's heads, and the adult, are visible.

May and Anna Murphy, Summerhill, were daughters of Head Constable Murphy, RIC. The orphanage given as the address for a few of the girls was run by the Sisters of Mercy. **Back** (l to r): May Murphy, Summerhill; Maureen Cooney; Tilly Coonan, Whitewalls; Kathleen Kelly, Turnpike; Fred Ryan, Carrigatoher; Josephine McGrath, Knigh; Mary Dillon, Tyone; Anna Murphy, Summerhill; Mary O'Meara, Rathurles. **3rd Row:** Nelly Dunne, The Orphanage; – Connors, Pound St; Maggie Jones; Jo Gaynor, Ballygraigue; Chrissie Kavanagh, The Orphanage; May Ryan, Ballycahill; Mary Hogan. **2nd Row:** Bridgie Hourigan, Birr Road; Aggie Reddan, Bachelor's Walk; Louise McGuigan, Turnpike; Susan Riordan, Capparoe; Mag Egan, do.; Mary Catherine Gleeson, Cudville; Patricia Powell, Cloughjordan & The Orphanage; Lily Talbot. **Front:** Cissie Ryan, Queen St; Nannie Fogarty, Barrack St; Mary Kate Kirwan, Ballycahill; Margaret Hogan, Cloughjordan & The Orphanage; Mary Kate Cawley; Peggie Dillon, Tyone; Mary Gleeson, Spout Road; Mary Spain, Moanfin.

132 (*above*) **St. Mary's Secondary School,** late 1930s. **Back** (l to r): Mary B. O'Brien, Carrigatoher; Sadie Devaney, Ballycommon; Christina Farrell, Scariff; Lena Delaney, Toomevara; Frances McNamara, Labasheeda; Mairéad O'Byrne, Roscrea; Statia Scroope, Cudville; Maura O'Brien, Ballina. **Middle:** Tessie Tierney, Gortlandroe; Maureen McCarthy, Silver St; Maureen Ryan, Mitchel St; Tess McSweeney, do.; Margaret Davy, Roscrea; Peg Seymour, Portroe. **Front:** Nancy Gleeson, Mitchel St; Bertha McCormack, Mitchel St; Eilish Cuddy, Wolfe Tone Tce; Biddy Darmody, Friar St; Joan Cadell, Kenyon St; Biddy Moylan, Rathnaleen; Bridie O'Meara, Kilruane.

It was the best of times, it was the worst of times, it was the age of wisdom, it was the age of foolishness, it was the epoch of belief, it was the epoch of incredulity, it was the season of Light, it was the season of Darkness, it was the spring of hope, it was the winter of despair, we had everything before us, we had nothing before us, we were all going direct to Heaven, we were all going direct the other way. – Charles Dickens, *A Tale of Two Cities* – and it may have been the tale of four schools.

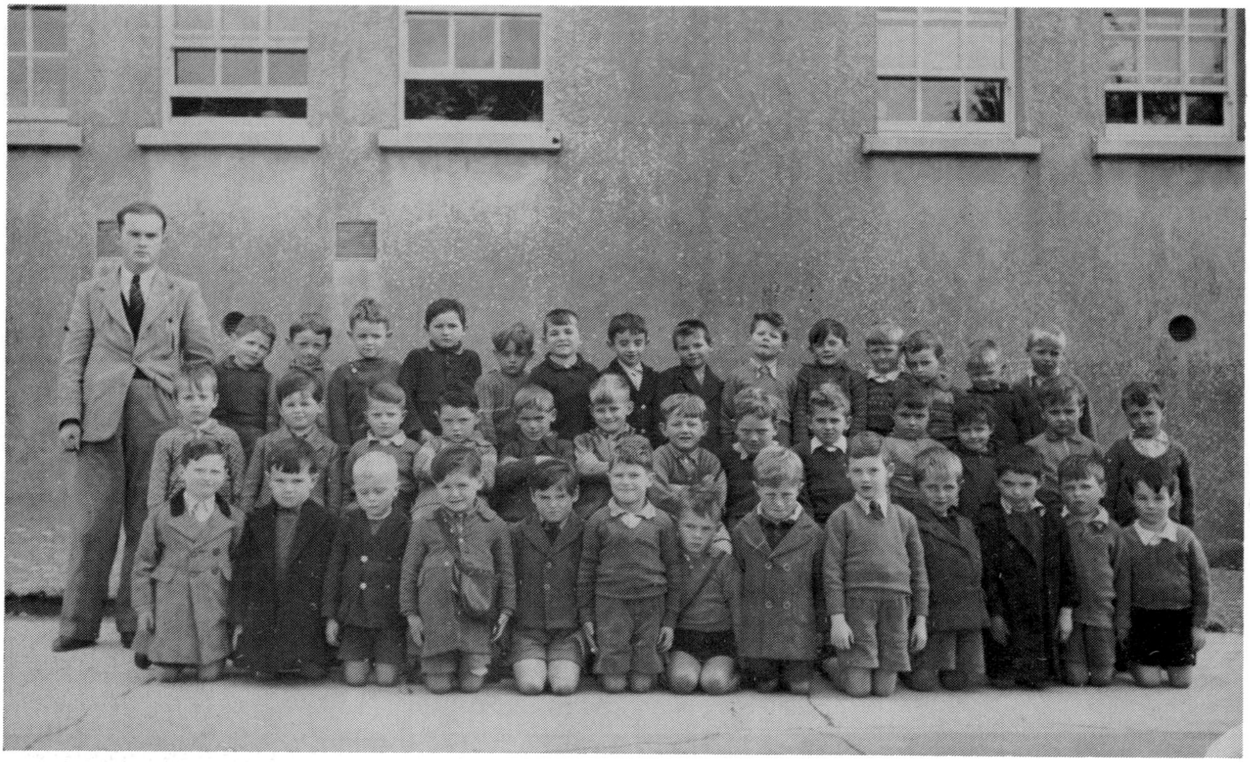

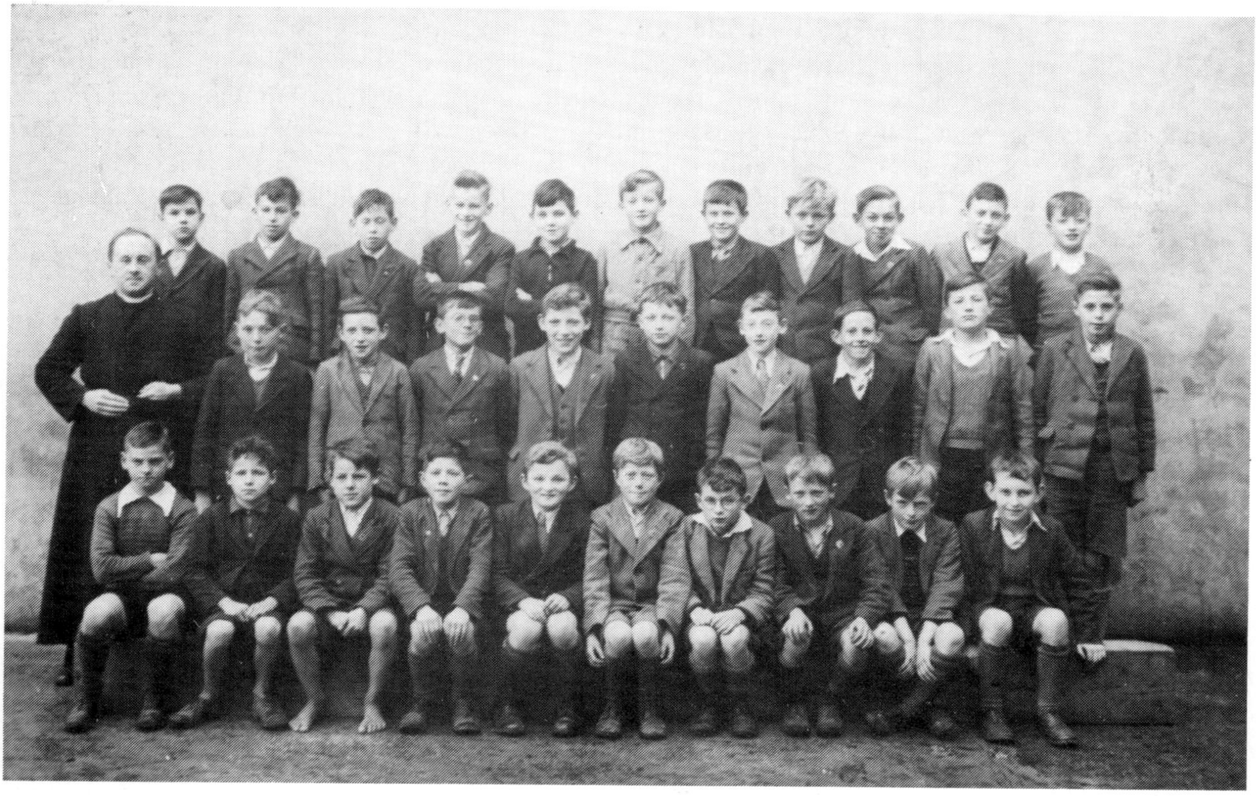

133 (*opposite, above*) **St. Mary's Boys National School,** late 1939 or early 1940. *The boys with names italicised below stayed together up to Inter Cert class, 1948-9.* Teacher: Mr McGrath. **Back** (l to r): Patrick McMahon, Jimmy Gleeson, Louis Murphy, John Harty, Laddens Hackett, Jimmy Sherlock, Noel Gleeson, Jim Duggan, Seán Naughton, *Ger Ryan*, - Bourke, *Jackie Gleeson*, Tommy McGowan, Francie Quigley. **Middle:** Paddy Kennedy, Morgan McNamara, Jimmy White, Terry Gleeson, Willie Sherlock, *Phil McGrath*, Sean Donnelly, Frank Donnelly, John Meagher, Michael Hynes, Paddy Joe Brett, Ger Gleeson, Pa Fitzpatrick. **Front:** Tommy Powell, – Hennebry, Brendan Heaslip, Tim Danagher, *Tony Fahy*, John McGrath, P. J. Kennedy, *Gerry McLoughlin*, *Donal Murphy*, Michael Hayes, Eddie Hynes, M. Ward, *Tony Hackett*. **40**

134 (*opposite, below*) **C.B.S. Primary School,** either 4th or 5th class, 1944 or 1945. *Italicised as above.* **Back** (l to r): Joe Quinlan, Christy Morgan, *Jim Barrett*, *Phil McGrath*, *Hubert Brennan*, Tim Frawley, Michael Connors, *Hugh Slattery*, *Ger Lewis*, *Ger Ryan*, Pa Fitzpatrick. **Middle:** Bro J. C. Hayes, Ned Meagher, Tony Ryan, Harold Ryan, Tony Healy, *Michael Ahearne*, *Donal Murphy*, Jimmy O'Grady, Noel Hyland, Vinnie Power. **Front:** *Tony Fahy*, Paddy Joe Brett, Willie Darmody, Patrick McMahon, *Gerry O'Dowd*, *Gerry McLoughlin*, Peter Lefébrè, Joe McGowan, Seamus Leahy, *Jackie Gleeson*. **34**

135 (*above*) **Leaving Cert Class 1951. Back** (l to r): Gerry McLoughlin, Wolfe Tone Tce; Tony Hackett, Sarsfield St; Liam Horgan, Silver St; Michael (Mickser) O'Connell, St. Flannan St; Hubert Brennan, Keeper View; Phil McGrath, Summerhill; Ger Ryan, Keeper View; Jackie Gleeson, MacDonagh St; Hugh Slattery, Ballyanny. **Front:** Gerry O'Dowd, Summerhill; Ger Lewis, MacDonagh Tce; Matt McGrath, Kenyon St; Michael Ahearne, Ormond St; Bob O'Leary, Beechwood; Donal Murphy, Pearse St. **15**

From the era before free post-primary education (1967-8) and compulsory attendance to age 15 (1972): just 16 of the 1939-40 class of 40 went forward, though not all in the same class or school, to complete the Intermediate Certificate eight or nine years on and the Leaving Certificate two years later. The class of 15 Leaving Certificate pupils was a record high then, as compared with 112 & 134 in two years of the 1990s. Just two went forward to third level. Four emigrated but returned, three of them to the Nenagh area. Three others migrated to Dublin but returned home.

136 CBS Confirmation Class c.1938. Back (l to r): Jack Murphy, Kenyon St; Jimmy Quigley, Birr Rd; Stephen Griffin, St. Joseph's Park; Christy O'Donnell, Summerhill; Eddie John McGrath, St. Flannan St; Micky Mason, St. Joseph's Park; Tony O'Connor, MacDonagh Tce; Joe Reynolds, do.; Dick McGrath, Yellow Bridge; John Chadwick, Tyone; Bertie Horan, St. Flannan St; Raymond Moloney, Summerhill; Joey Brereton, Sarsfield St; Seán Kennedy, Abbey St; Neil Frawley, Rathmartin; Tony Hassett, Tyone; – . **3rd Row:** Bro Doody, CBS; Niall Gleeson, Keeper View; Frank Lewis, MacDonagh Tce; Jim Murray, Sarsfield St; Paddy Coleman, Tyone; Denis Carey, Sarsfield St; Eddie Kinirons, do.; Finn O'Driscoll, Newtown; Milo Magee, Silver St; Seán Fahy, Wolfe Tone Tce; Tim Quinlan, Ciamalta Rd; Seán Slattery, Pearse St; Dick White, Silver St; Pilib Cleary, Church Rd; Dan Egan, Gortlandroe; Jim Freeman, St. John's Tce; Eamonn Fleming, Kenyon St; Raphael Gleeson, Cloughjordan. **2nd Row:** John O'Grady, Abbey St; 'Balf' O'Brien, Sarsfield St; Michael Cleary, Silver St; Kieran O'Gorman, Church Rd; Joe O'Connor, Silver St; Johnny Gill, Summerhill; Tony Ryan, Kenyon St; Tony Morrissey, Summerhill; Noel Jones, St. Flannan St; Billy Kennedy, William St; Tony Whelan, Rossa Place; John Hogan, MacDonagh St; Matt Whelan, Kyle; Albie Manning, Gortlandroe; Christy Ryan, Richmond; Jimmy Tidd, Sarsfield St; Tommy Tobin, Sarsfield St. **Front:** Vincie O'Connor, MacDonagh Tce; Martin Ryan, Kenyon St; Jack Freeman, St. John's Tce; Liam Ray, St. Patrick's Tce; Jackie Spearman, Ormond St; Jossie Whelan, Rossa Place; Ger Ryan, Mitchel St; Liam White, Silver St; Eamonn Lee, St. Patrick's Tce; Paddy Guilfoyle, Tullaheady; Joe Flannery, MacDonagh Tce; Denis Sheahan, Kenyon Street; Michael McGrath, Pearse St; Frankie O'Connor, MacDonagh Tce; Paddy McLoughlin, St. Joseph's Park; Buddy Shoer, do.; Ger Moroney, Ciamalta Road; Michael Geaney, Clare St.

137 (*above*) **Nenagh CBS,** 1951 winners of the Croke Cup for Co. Tipperary schools. **Back** (l to r): Pierce O'Leary, Beechwood; Seamus Cleary, Dromcolliher, Co. Limerick, & Annbrook; Paddy Hallinan, Knockalton; Tony (Jack) Burns, St. John's Tce; Jimmy Foley, Summerhill; Ger O'Connor, Sarsfield St; Ger McCarthy, Silver St; Seamus Ryan, Sarsfield St; Andrew McDonnell, Grallagh; Oliver McGrath, Summerhill. **Front**: George Sheahan, Silvermines; Sean Nealon, Newtown; Mick Burns, St. John's Tce; Tony Hackett (Captain) Sarsfield St; Michael Gilmartin, Kenyon St; Tom Harris, Pearse St; Liam Gleeson, Ballintotty. Burns, Gilmartin and Hallinan represented Tipperary at All-Ireland minor level; Burns graduated to win five senior All-Irelands, six National Leagues, four Oireachtas, an inter-provincial Railway Cup and two St. Brendan's Cup wins against New York. O'Connor later won an All-Ireland Youths Discus title. Gleeson became Nenagh Olympic A.C.'s first Hon Sec and multiple champion (see pages 82 & 116).

138 (*left*) **St. Mary's Secondary School on Top.** There were three unique aspects to the Irish Schools athletics finals, 1979. St. Mary's had already been the first school to win all three relays at the 1978 finals. They repeated this in 1979 with a Duggan sister on each of the three teams – (l to r) Lelia, Margaret and Claire – and Noelle Morrissey running the anchor leg for all three. The full teams were Junior: C Duggan, Mary McKenna, Noreen Murphy, N Morrissey; Inter: Carmel Maher, L Duggan, Fidelma White, N Morrissey; Senior: M Duggan, Alice McKenna, N Murphy, N Morrissey.

139 (*left*) **Frank McGrath's** (seated) lifespan of almost eighty years was filled with achievement. As a hurler he won two North Tipperary championship medals with his native Youghalarra-Burgess (1908, 1909); three county championships with Toomevara Greyhounds, 1912-14, under the captaincy of Widger Meagher; the North championship with Nenagh, 1915. As administrator, he served as chairman of the North GAA Board, 1922-3 and 1927-33; chairman of the Munster Council; chairman of the Committee which oversaw the purchase and development of MacDonagh Park, Nenagh, 1941-2.

Frank McGrath was manager of the very successful Tipperary hurling team which toured the United States in 1926. His cordial personality, dedication and efficiency come across in Thomas J. Kenny's published diary of the tour, of which an edited extract is in *Tipperary: A Treasure Chest* (RELAY, 1995).

He was also an accomplished handballer. He introduced stepdancing to the Nenagh branch of the Gaelic League in 1917.

He was O/C 1st Tipperary Brigade of the Irish Republican Army, and a judge in the Sinn Féin courts, during the War of Independence,1919-21. He served two terms of imprisonment in English jails – Durham in 1919, and Wormwood Scrubbs in 1920.

He had a bar & grocery at 56 Castle/Pearse St, and a corn and wool stores in Peter/Kickham St. He lived at various times in Idrone Cottage, Dromin, and 24 Summerhill. He was married to Bea Meagher, Annfield, Thurles. His sons Eddie John, Brendan, Phil and Oliver appear in hurling photographs in this volume. Frank died in Dublin in 1965 and is buried in Lisboney cemetery.

The North Tipperary Board, of which he was President, named their championship trophy in his honour. This year (1996) the Frank McGrath Cup rests on a Newport sideboard for the first time ever.

Frank McGrath's protégé in the photograph is **Rody Nealon** (1898-1988), Newtown. They were in Dublin for a Feis competition. As compensation for defeat Frank bought Rody a handball and took him to have his photograph taken. The picture captures the air of confidence of both, and some similarity of dress for man and boy. Rody is aged about 12 years, thus placing the date as c.1910. Rody also became a hurler and administrator. He played senior hurling with Counties Waterford, Kilkenny and Tipperary, winning an All-Ireland junior with Tipp in 1924, and a senior in 1925. He also had the distinction in 1924 of playing for Ireland in the Tailteann Games. He was a member of the McGrath-managed US touring hurling team of 1926. He was Chairman of the North Board 1924-7, and a later President.

Rody followed the profession of his father and uncle – national school teacher. He taught in his native Youghalarra parish for close on forty years. He was succeeded by his son Donal who has won national recognition on the treble – firstly, as winner of five All-Ireland senior hurling titles with Tipperary between 1958 and 1965 and a Caltex hurling award in 1962; secondly, as coach and one of the troika (with Michael 'Babs' Keating and Theo English) responsible for the Tipperary team which won the All-Ireland in 1989 after a gap of seventeen years; thirdly, as Munster Council secretary.

140 (*right*) **Pádraig Ó Meadhra, M.A. (1905-1971)** was born in Grawn, Toomevara. He trained as a national teacher in St Patrick's College, Dublin, and taught in Nenagh CBS until he took over the principalship of St Mary's Boys N.S. in 1967. Outside of the classroom his energies were directed into the Irish language movement, Conradh na Gaeilge, Irish dancing, music and literature, and the acquisition of the North Tipperary Club building for the local Conradh headquarters, re-named Dún Mhuire. As owner of Cló Uí Mheára, Aonach Urmhumhan, he published books and schools text in Irish. He was editor of the *Nenagh Guardian*, 1942-45, to which he contributed a regular column; co-editor, with his brother-in-law, Tomás MacDomhnaill, of *The Spirit of Tipperary* – an anthology of verse in Irish and English; and writer of several pageants for his innovative St Patrick's night concerts.

141 (*left*) **Thomas J. McGrath (1920-82)** was born in St. Flannan's St, Nenagh, and educated locally. He joined the post office and served in Birr and Nenagh before his appointment as Postmaster in Nenagh in 1969 – the position he held at the time of his death in February 1982.

Tom's commitment to involvement in community effort was manifested in his membership of Tipperary (NR) Vocational Committee, of which he was chairman for twenty-three years; Nenagh Boat Club (Hon Sec for thirty-four years); Ormond Anglers; Parish Council; Nenagh Castle Restoration Committee (Hon. Treasurer); and the Scouts Hall Committee. He had a keen interest in local history and contributed fishing, historical and other articles to *The Guardian* and *Cois Deirge*.

Tom married Marguerite Ryan, Roscrea, and they had one son and five daughters. In 1958 they moved from St. Flannan's St to the former Dempsey home, Drom an Ailtigh, beside MacDonagh Park. Notwithstanding the change of name in 1920, the McGrath family continue to use the older name of Whitewalls Road as their address.

142 (*right*) **Edward Joseph Conway (1894-1968)**, M.D., MRIA, FRS, D. Sc., FRCPI, FRIC, FRSA, born at No. 4 Queen/Mitchel St, son of William Francis and Mary (née McCready). He received his early education at the Christian Brothers School in John's Lane. He qualified as a medical doctor and later became an outstanding biophysicist and originator of microdiffusion analsysis (a method for measuring the amount of oxygen in the bloodstream).

He was appointed the first Professor of Biochemistry and Pharmacology at University College Dublin – and served for thirty years, 1934-64. His scholarship brought him many honours including the Boyle Medal of the Royal Dublin Society in 1967. He wrote two books and contributed articles to leading international scientific journals.

143 (*left*) **Peter Dempsey, OFM Cap.** was born in Nenagh on 14 September 1914, baptised as Rory. His father, Paul Dempsey, was the first Chief Executive Officer of North Tipperary Vocational Committee. He was educated in Nenagh CBS and the Cistercian College, Roscrea. He entered the Capuchin Order and took the name Peter. He was ordained in September 1939. He then went to Rome where he obtained an L.S.S.from the Biblical Institute (1943) and an S.T.L. from the Gregorian. Returning to Ireland, he got an M.A. degree from the National University. Further honours were a Masters degree in Psychology and a Ph.D. from Montreal, Canada. He became a lecturer at University College Cork, in 1952. He set up the Department of Applied Psychology where he was Professor until his retirement in 1982. Doctors Conway and Dempsey both returned to roots in the mid-Sixties as lecturers in a series organised by William J Heaney for Nenagh branch of Muintir na Tíre in the Ormond Hotel.

144 (*left*) Pilib Ó Cléirig, Church Road and Mitchel St, with the trophy named 'Corn Uí Cléirig' presented in January 1973 to North Tipp Bord na n-Óg, for the u/14 football championship in that division. Pilib was a tireless worker for Conradh na Gaeilge and the GAA until his untimely death in 1982 at the age of 55.

145 (*below*) An Taoiseach, Eamon de Valera (3rd from left), in 1958, enjoying a break away from duties, in his usual Nenagh stop over – the Carmel Hotel, Summerhill. With him are (l to r): Jim Watkins, Dublin, a vet with Jack Powell, Summerhill; Very Rev. Edmund Murphy, P.P., Silvermines, Rev. Michael Hillery, C.C., Nenagh.

146 The Carey Brothers, reflected in one of their own products for a Nenagh Chamber of Commerce publication, *Why Nenagh For Your Industry?* 1981. **Behind** (l to r): Gus, Willie. **Front:** Seamus. In 1965 the Templederry-born brothers launched in Silver St, Nenagh, what is now the very successful Carey Bros, VistaTherm Glass. Five years later they transferred to their purpose-built premises on the Limerick road. Business and premises have been a-growing since. Their horizons became European in 1993 with the acquisition of a British Standard. This was followed by their being the first Irish firm in their field to be awarded an international management certificate. Employment figures have grown to 260 (1996). Their glass products are exported to most European countries.

147 (*left*) In 1974 the residents of St. Joseph's Park took the initiative to provide and furnish a children's playground on a site purchased by themselves. They named it St. Paul's Playground to mark the encouragement given them by Mother M. Paul Leahy of the Convent of Mercy. A hardworking Committee fund-raised intensively to get the project going. **Back** (l to r): Bill O'Brien, Michael Cummins, Tom Ray, James Hogan. **Front:** Chrissie Morgan, Aggie Bourke, Kathleen Cummins.

148 (*below*) Twenty-six years on it is now patronised by their grandchildren, and by the children of those who were enjoying the 'roundabout' when the photographer called. The adults in the picture are (l to r): John McCullough; Mary Kate Creagh, Kathleen Cummins.

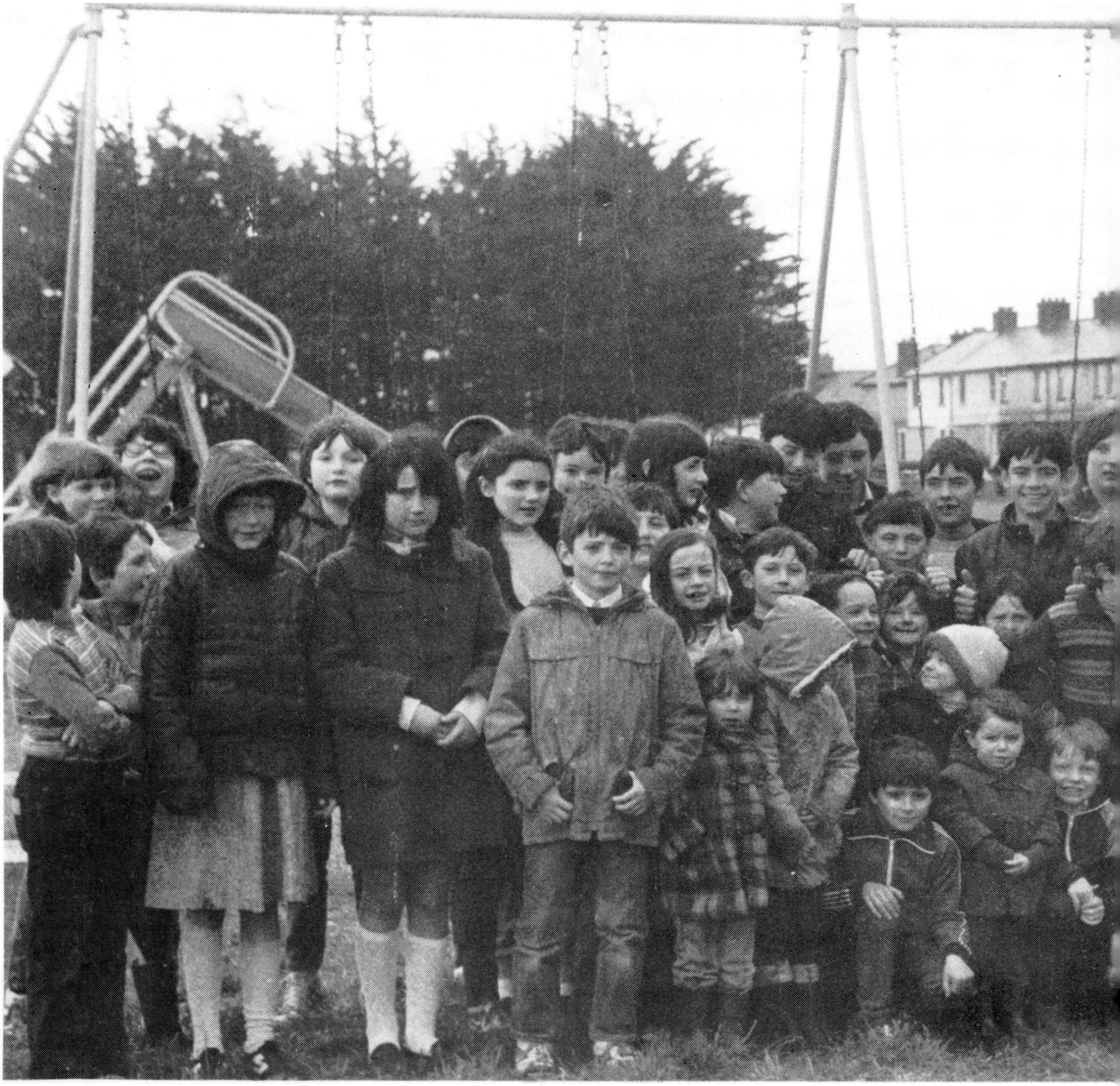

1
2
3
4
5
6
7
8
9
10
11
12
13
14
15
16
17
18
19
20
21
22
23
24
25
26
27
28
29
30
31
32
33
34
35
36
37
38
39
40
41
42
43
44
45
46
47
48
49
50
51
52
53
54
55
56
57
58
59
60
61
62

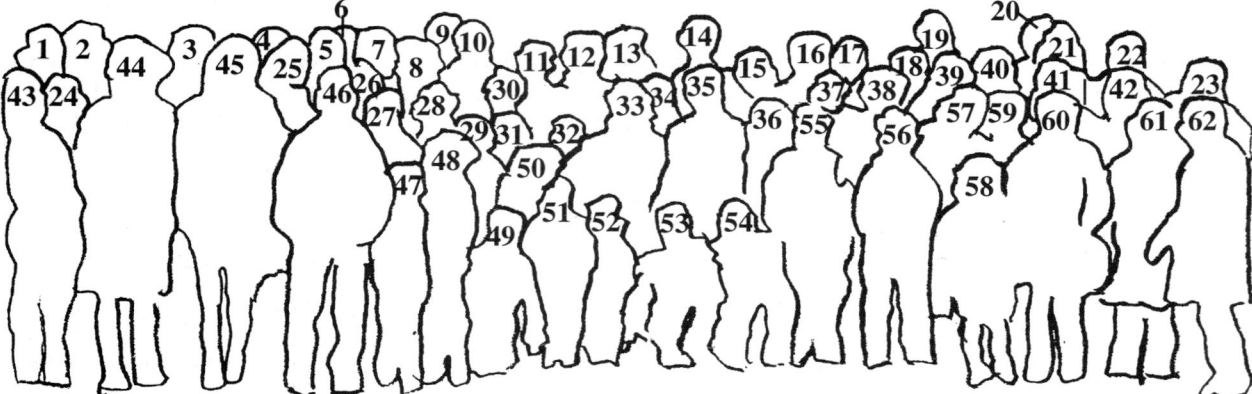

149 Patrons of St. Paul's Playground with Sr Assumpta Kearns, St. Mary's Secondary School, in the 1980s. The children are from neighbouring St Joseph's Park. 1 – , 2 – , 3 Shirley Finn, 4 – , 5 Margaret Butler, 6 – , 7 Claire Lawlor, 8 Seánie O'Brien, 9 David Lawlor, 10 Patsy O'Brien, 11 Mark White, 12 Brian Mitchell, 13 Elizabeth Walsh, 14 Denis Finn, 15 Thomas McCarthy, 16 Sr Assumpta Kearns, 17 David Walsh, 18 – , 19 – , 20 – , 21 Tracey Shoer, 22 David White, 23 Deirdre Tully, 24 Catherine Looney, 25 Margaret Griffin, 26 Stephen Griffin, 27 Sandra White, 28 Robbie Lawlor, 29 Darren Mitchell, 30 Don Mitchell, 31 Marie Walsh, 32 Patricia Tomlinson, 33 John Walsh, 34 – , 35 Michael Walsh, 36 Ger Tanner, 37 Theresa O'Meara, 38 Tom O'Meara, 39 Martina Shoer, 40 Pauline Creagh, 41 Margaret O'Brien, 42 Ann McGrath, 43 Denise Ryan, 44 Janette Ryan, 45 Martina Donnellan, 46 – , 47 Audrey Hourigan, 48 – , 49 – , 50 – , 51 – , 52 Paul Corbett, 53 Jason Butler, 54 Michael McGrath, 55 Tony Kennedy, 56 Peter Daly, 57 Sandra Shoer, 58 Sasha Ryan, 59 – , 60 Stephanie Griffin, 61 Edel Butler, 62 Geraldine O'Brien.

150 Nenagh Cycling Club 1901. The invention of the pneumatic tyre by John Dunlop, Belfast, in 1887 revolutionised the bicycle. A cycling club was founded in Nenagh in 1894. Members went on organised 'runs' on Sundays.

There is a fine contingent of females in this group setting out from Peter Street. They are undeterred by the long skirt which was the fashion of that time. Cycling became the 'in' thing in the mid-1890s, with the female cyclist attracting much attention. French fashion designers created some daring outfits, including variations on the bloomers. Once the British royal ladies took to the bike the market boomed – even extending to 'cycling academies' where, bike owner or not, you could learn to cycle.

Versifier Sergeant Jack Keily, RIC, observed the phenomenon and recorded it in September 1895 for regular readers of his contributions to the *Nenagh News*.

'Twas vain to say we had no funds
A 'solid-tyre' to buy,
If we did not procure a 'bike'
She'd nothing do but cry!
To grudge the price – a pound or two!
Was miserably mean,
So we had to yield, and now she rides
A solid-tyre machine!

Now Mary's mother used a wheel,
But 'twas for spinning flax,
And when we tell our daughter this,
Oh, Lord, how fierce she'll wax;
It's from the present not the past
Her knowledge she will glean,
And so she'll enter Parliament
Upon her new machine!

Women were granted the vote for local government elections in 1898, and for general elections in 1918, but it was then confined to women over the age of thirty.

151 *(left)* **Riverdale Pitch-and-Putt Course**, photographed by a leading member, Johnny Shoer, built on the site of a former dump at Kylera beside the Ollatrim river, one mile out on the 'Old' Birr road. The dump, itself in a former quarry, was initially filled with two hundred lorry loads of soil and rubble from the new Yewston estate.

Riverdale Club was founded on 25 June 1973 in the Loreto Hall, Kenyon St. The founder members were: Johnny Nagle, Chairman, Silver View; Michael Morgan, vice-Chairman, Bulfin Crescent; John O'Riordan, Hon Sec, Kickham St; Joint Hon Treasurers: Mrs Ann Gaffney, Bulfin Crescent, and Mrs Phil Nagle, Silver View; Billy Gaffney, Captain, Bulfin Crescent; Committee: Noel Bowler, Hanly's Place; Tony Healy, Sallygrove; Willie Hyde, Pound Rd; Patrick Kennedy, Sallygrove; Paddy Lawlor, Sallygrove; George McLean, Sallygrove; Billy Morgan, Annbrook Heights; Jack Nagle, Clare St; Arthur Smith, Old Birr Rd/ Bulfin Rd.

Riverdale became the first County Tipperary club to win a Munster title – in 1994, and they duplicated this feat in 1996. One member, Seán Minogue, also an Éire Óg hurler and official, has represented Ireland – versus Australia in 1996, earning the runner-up individual prize.

152 *(left)* **Show Committee** members count the takings at the Show Dance in the Scouts Hall. **Standing** (l to r): Alfie O'Brien, Bayly Farm, Ballinaclough; Harry Howard, Ballymackey; Stan Gubbins, Pearse St; Mick O'Meara, Melrose; Dan O'Sullivan (Secretary), Kickham St; Ned Gleeson, Mitchel St. **Seated:** J. B. (Barney) O'Driscoll, Newtown; Dr Tony Courtney, Summerhill.

153 Nenagh Ormond Rugby Football Club, 1983–4 u18 County, O'Donovan Cup and North Munster League winners. **Back:** Noel O'Meara (Fixtures Sec), Gortlandroe; Michael Hackett (Juveniles delegate), Bawn; Dan Hickey, Silvermines; Philip Whelan, Ballygraigue; Paul Spain, Limerick Rd; Donal O'Brien, Annbrook Heights; Denis O'Meara, Ballintotty; Albert Purcell, Puckane; Noel Coffey, St. Flannan's St; Peg Morgan (PRO), Richmond; Teddy Morgan (team manager & coach), do. **Middle:** Fergal Healy (trainer), Rapla; Jim McGrath, St. Joseph's Park; Eamonn Morgan, Richmond; Noel O'Meara, Sallygrove; Ger Morris, Limerick Rd; Ger Lewis (Club President), Knight's Crescent; Martin Hynes (Capt), Benedine; Christy Morgan, St. Joseph's Park; Kieran O'Brien, Annbrook Heights; Paul Delaney, Knockanpierce; Dr Tom Hayes (coach), Melrose. **Front:** David Nevin, St. Joseph's Park; Liam Ryan, Summerhill; Paul Collins, Monaree; Paul Nevin, St. Joseph's Park. **Absent:** Charlie Monaghan, Puckane.

That O'Donovan Cup Final

Could the setting have been better? Thomond Park in May 1984. Nenagh Ormonds' last match of the season and of their century; a huge crowd of supporters ranging from veterans of the Thirties to the parents and friends of the under 18s on the pitch for the final of the O'Donovan Cup, the prestige competition for North Munster juveniles.

These Nenagh lads have been unbeaten through 19 games this season. They had beaten Clanwilliam in the county final for the Martin O'Sullivan Cup on the previous day. Four players are carrying injuries.

With moments to go, Shannon are leading by 6 points to Nenagh's 3 – a Jim McGrath penalty. Leg-weary they may be but the brains are ticking over. Liam Ryan takes a quick throw-in; Denis O'Meara collects at the end of a thin line, gets it to Charlie Monaghan; into a ruck. Donie O'Brien heels the ball smartly, his brother Kieran at scrum-half slings it to out-half Jim McGrath who goes for a drop goal.

It is charged down by the alert Shannon boys on the verge of a first Cup success, also within their centenary year. But McGrath collects it and flings a long pass to winger Paul Collins whose speed and determination takes him across the line near the corner. 7-6. Delirium; the final whistle; a most dignified acceptance speech by captain Martin Hynes. He acknowledges the management by Peg and Teddy Morgan and the coaching over the years and over the season.

These lads have had a plethora of success since assembled as under 12s – and some set-backs. They have had the benefit of coaching from Teddy, Stephen Mitchell, Seamus Burns and Tom Hayes. They have been mothered by Peg, who indeed has a son, Eamonn, in the squad.

– from the chapter, 'Mol an Óige', in *Nenagh Ormond's Century 1884-1984*.

That extraordinary record for the season was (F=friendly, L=league), Nenagh scores first in each case: versus – Rockwell College (F), 4-4; Rockwell College (F), 6-6; Young Munster (F), 0-0; Birr (F), 24-16; Birr (F), 18-16; Cork Constitution (F), 7-0; Newcastlewest (L), 12-0; Richmond (L), 24-6; Garryowen (L), 10-0; Castleisland (L), 22-4; Newcastlewest (L. Final), 28-3; Thomond (N.M. cup), 29-0; Young Munster (N.M. cup), 24-0; Shannon (N.M. cup final), 7-6; Visitors XV (F), 4-3; Clanwilliam (F), 4-3; County Selected XV (F), 14-0; Ealing-London (F), 13-16; Cashel (county semi-final), 10-3; Clanwilliam (county final), 32-8.

Some longer-term results of the dedicated coaching have been: N O'Meara, with Young Munsters, and Spain, with Garryowen, both won All-Ireland League titles. Spain also got three senior and one junior Munster caps. Himself and E Morgan won u20 Munster League with Garryowen. K O'Brien played u20 with Connacht and senior with Athlone; he was a sub on an Irish RTCs team versus Wales. McGrath and Purcell played some senior with Bohemians and Hickey with Crescent. P Nevin, K O'Brien and N O'Meara, joined by Tony Gregan, played on a Munster u18 team on the same day. D Nevin also got a Munster u18 cap. The squad later furnished three Club Captains – N O'Meara, Spain and Jim McGrath, himself the son of a onetime club captain and athlete, Michael McGrath (see page 82). Later brothers-in-law Coffey and D O'Brien were part of the Éire Óg squad which won Nenagh's first county hurling championship in 1995. D O'Brien represented Tipperary at u12 Community Games finals at Mosney.

154 (*above*) **Camogie Team Aonach Urmhumhan, 1918.** In 1918 the groundswell of support for Sinn Féin included locally an active branch of Cumann na mBan. Their activities embraced the formation of a camogie club who played against Roscrea as part of an Aeríocht in June. It has not been possible to identify the individuals in the photograph.

155 (*below*) **Nenagh's First GAA Co. Champions** – the Nenagh Institute footballers of 1911. They beat Ballinaclough, Youghal, Templemore, Tipperary O'Learys (the reigning county champions) on route to a county final draw against Thurles. Before the replay could take place Templetuohy defeated Thurles in the Mid final and represented Mid against Nenagh who won. Nenagh Institute won again in 1915. The 1911 team (not individually identified in the photograph): Tim Whealey (Captain); Maurice Foley, John Walsh, John and Pat Costello, Mick Scannell, Mick Egan, Frank and Willie Flannery, Martin Clifford, Jim Moore, Charlie Spain, Ned Kennedy, Jack Nolan, Tom Smyth, William Flannery, Pat O'Meara, J. Ryan.

156 Nenagh Éire Óg Senior Hurlers – the full panel of players prior to the North Final against Roscrea at Borrisokane on 1 Aug 1982. **Back** (l to r): Pat Lee, P. J. Maxwell, Ger O'Brien, Conor Ryan, Jim Nagle, Michael Kennedy, Liam Heffernan, Michael Ryan, John Flannery, Michael Griffin, Conor O'Donovan, John Tucker, Mattie Ryan, John Darcy. **Front:** Jim O'Sullivan, Seán Minogue, Máirtín O'Connor, Brian Heffernan, Denis Finnerty, Christy Tucker, John Heffernan, Philip Kennedy, Roger Coffey, Seamus Kennedy (goalie), Phil Hennessy, Robert Ashman, Paul Kennedy, Pat Power.

It was a clash laden with a full hour's tension, excitement and entertainment, which gradually built up to a heart-stopping climax. Both sides balanced the levelling scales no less than six times and the score gap between them only ever widened to a maximum of four points … – The Guardian.

Éire Óg, who had beaten Borrisoleigh and Silvermines, drew with Roscrea, 0–17 to 3–8, in this attempt to win a fourth North title. The replay was put on hold while the county quarter finals were got out of the way. In these Éire Óg drew with Moycarkey on 8 August, but were defeated in the replay on the following Sunday. The North Final replay was fixed for 29 August. However, Nenagh withdrew in protest against a Co. Board directive involving players also due to play the All-Ireland minor final on 5 Sept. This in effect gave Roscrea the postponement they sought from 29 August, claiming four injured players, but perceived by Éire Óg as 'a cover-up for the real reason, namely, the dismissal of two of their members by the referee' in the county semi-final on 20 Aug. The Co. Board had previously refused Éire Óg, injury-stricken, a postponement of the Moycarkey replay (their fourth successive Sunday on field). The outcome was: no final, no North champions, and another decade till Nenagh's fourth title.

Thirteen of the panel had been among the county minor champion squads, 1977 and 1978. Five survived the thirteen-year span to 1995 to feature in the town's first ever county senior hurling title – O'Donovan & J Heffernan (meantime All-Ireland winners with Tipp, 1989 & 91 and 1989, respectively), Finnerty (All-Ireland minor winner, 1980, and sharing in six successive county wins, 1977 & 78 minor, 1979-82 u21, as did Lee), Hennessy and Paul Kennedy. The club had meantime won North titles, 1992, 93, those five players and Philip Kennedy sharing in the 1992 win after a twenty-eight year gap.

157 (*above*) **Sarsfields, Nenagh**, 1944-45-46, finalists in the North Tipperary Junior Championship, 1945. **Back:** Tom Bourke, Wolfe Tone Tce; Tomás Costello, Sarsfield St; Martin Ryan, Kenyon St; Joe Slattery, MacDonagh St; Brendan McGrath, Summerhill; Frank Lewis, MacDonagh Tce; Eddie McGrath, Sarsfield St; Dan Nolan, Ciamalta Rd; Seán Slattery, Silver St; Tony Ryan, Kenyon St; Dan Costello, Sarsfield St. **Middle:** John Whelan, Sarsfield St; Pat Guilmartin, Silver St; Frank Manley, Wolfe Tone Tce; Thomas (Toddy) Shoer, Richmond; Tommy (Digger) Stanley, Sarsfield St; Christy Hackett, do. **Front:** Tom Brophy, Mitchel St; Michael Geaney, Clare St; Ger Costello, Wolfe Tone Tce; Paddy Bourke, do.

158 (*opposite, above*) **St. Mary's Minor Hurlers**, North Tipp champions, 1949. **Back** (l to r): Philip Hynes, William St; Stephen Ryan, St. Joseph's Park; Michael McLoughlin, Summerhill; Pat Hynes, William St; Paddy Carey, Sarsfield St; Willie Gleeson, Silver View; Reuben Butler, Rly Station Hse; Michael Doyle, Summerhill. **Middle:** Liam McKenna, Ballintoher, Chairman; Francis Fleming, Kenyon St; Michael Hynes, William St; Vincent Power, Summerhill; Sean O'Connell, St. Flannan's St; John Fleming, Kenyon St; Michael (Mickser) O'Connell, St. Flannan's St; Eddie Hynes, William St. **Front:** Barry Murphy, Kenyon St; Phil McGrath, Summerhill.

159 (*opposite, below*) **St Mary's Minor Footballers**, 1950. St Mary's won the North Tipp Minor Football title four years in a row, 1948-51. **Back** (l to r): Frank O'Donnell, Hon Sec, Silver St; Donal Murphy, Pearse St; Patrick Naughton, do.; Jimmy Cahill, Limerick Rd; Billy O'Brien, St. Flannan's St; Jerry Moloney, Ballyphilip; Mickey Spain, Sarsfield St; Christy Morgan, St. Joseph's Park; Liam McKenna, Ballintoher, Chairman. **Middle:** Willie Burns, Tobar Mhuire; Ger Lewis, MacDonagh Tce; Stephen Kelly, St. Joseph's Park; Willie Gleeson, Silver View; Mickser O'Connell, St. Flannan's St; Johnny Sheehy, Ballyphilip. **Front:** John Lawlor, Islandbawn; Philip Hynes, William St; Michael Fogarty, Keeper View; Donie O'Brien, Ballintotty; Phil McGrath, Summerhill; Johnny Gleeson, Mill Rd/Ormond St.

(See 157-9) 'After many vain attempts, Rev. Joe Hayes, C.C., succeeded in healing the breach that existed between Éire Óg' [NY 102] 'and the other Nenagh club, Sarsfields' [see 157]. 'There followed a great string of successes for Nenagh teams. Minor hurling honours were won 1947-48-49-51 and the Club was invariably well represented on Tipperary Minor selections. Jack Nolan, Billy and Donie O'Brien, Brendan and Phil McGrath, Michael O'Connell, Michael Hynes, Alec Reid, Johnny McGrath, Harry Sheehy, Paddy Hallinan, DeVere Reynolds, Edmund McGrath, Michael O'Shaughnessy, Mike Burns, Phil Hennessy, Páidi Kennedy, Michael Gilmartin have all represented their county since 1946 and the majority of them have won All-Ireland honours.' – *Nenagh: Irelands' Town of Champions* (1958). St. Mary's subsequently re-named itself Éire Óg under which name it won the town's first senior hurling North title in forty-two years, in 1957. It is now generally described as Nenagh Éire Óg or Éire Óg, Nenagh. (see also pages 111, 125)

160 (*above*) **The revived MacDonagh A.C. Open Sports**, 1952, three years before the athletes seceded and formed Nenagh Olympic A.C. **Back** (l to r): – Brosnan, Limerick; Jack Naughton; Patrick J. Kennedy, Killyloughnane, vice-Chairman; Mick Kennedy, Co. Board, Thurles; – ; Bro. J.T. Harris, Superior, CBS; Pat Grey, Whitewalls; John Nolan, Thurles; Paddy Maher, Summerhill, Hon Sec, Park Committee; Mick Brosnan, Limerick; Matt McGrath, Curraghmore; David O'Keeffe, Pearse St; Joe McGowan, St. Joseph's Park; Bobby Morgan, Birr Road; Jack Roberts, Whitewalls, MacDonagh Park Groundsman; Jackie Whelan, Summerhill; 2 boys: Michael O'Brien, MacDonagh St; Donal Whelan, Summerhill. **Middle:** Oliver Naughton, Pearse St; Martin Bourke, Sarsfield St; Seán Naughton; Joe Mahony, Handicapper-Starter, Dundrum; Bob Tisdall, 1932 400 hurdles Olympic champion, who presented the prizes; Donal Murphy, Hon Sec. **Front:** Patrick Naughton; Dan Murphy, Pearse St; Willie Cartwright, Provincial Bank; Tommy Costello, Sarsfield St, Hon Treas; Dinny O'Brien, Grange, Chairman. It was Bob Tisdall's first visit home since 1932. He was then farming 130 acres of coffee and 300 acres of wheat on his 'Tipperary Estate' in Tanganyika. He named his daughter, Nena. He now lives north of Brisbane, Queensland.

161 (*right*) **The First Juvenile All-Ireland for Nenagh Olympic**, 1974, on a wet day at Gormanston College in the national BLOE u14 relay final. (l to r): M O'Meara, Belleen; P Costello, Summerhill; N O'Grady, Tyone; and M Moroney, Bulfin Crescent. The three rings in the banner signify the three Olympic champions with local affiliations – Bob Tisdall, Matt McGrath, and Johnny Hayes.

Then Margaret O'Meara flew the first leg
For the girls not yet fourteen;
Patricia Costello scorched the earth
In a speed not quite foreseen;

Margaret Moroney sped the bend
To leave Nenagh in second place,
Till Nora O'Grady swept into the lead
Twenty metres from the tape.

162 (*right*) **Seven Chiefs and One Relay Team**, winners on a sunny day at Waterford, 1974. **Back:** Donal Murphy, coach; Nancy Murphy, Hon Treas; Seán Naughton, Tony Hassett, Tom Holmes, Patrick Naughton, coaches; John Quill, Chairman. **Front:** Mary McKenna, Ballintoher; Claire Duggan, Benedine; Lorna Moroney, Bulfin Crescent; Caroline Kinane, Toomevara.

163 (*left*) **Gold, Silver & Bronze**, 1976. **Back:** Denis Finnerty, Ballygraigue Rd; Michael Morrissey, Monsea; John Cody, Kenyon St; Kieran O'Brien, Lisboney; John Guinan, Lorrha. **Front:** Noreen Murphy, Ballinaclogh; Bríd Naughton, Tyone; Lelia Duggan, Benedine; Noelle Morrissey, Monsea; Lorna Moroney, national high jump champion. The other four girls hold the unique record of seven national relay titles in a row, 1975-81, u11-17. D Finnerty later broke the Irish junior hurdles record three times. Eight of the ten competed for Ireland in senior and/or junior and/or schools internationals. [NY 116]

164 (*left*) **Record Breakers Meet.** Liam Gleeson (see page 82) and Maeve Kyle, Ballymena, who still holds the world veterans' record for 400 metres in two age groups. She competed for Ireland in the Olympic Games and for Northern Ireland in the Commonwealth Games and was also a hockey international. Liam captained Ireland, having been a founder and first Hon Sec of Nenagh Olympic.

165, 166 (*middle*) Maeve Kyle was the guest of honour and presented the prizes at Nenagh Olympic's 1977 social. Patricia Costello (left) and Alice McKenna (right) received bronze for the BLOE national u16 relay. In 1976 Patricia shared the u16 title with Nora O'Grady, Mary O'Halloran and Ann Murphy. Alice McKenna shared the u15 win with Patricia, Evelyn Gleeson and Ann Murphy. Each 1976 title was won in a new record, 52.0 and 50.7, respectively.

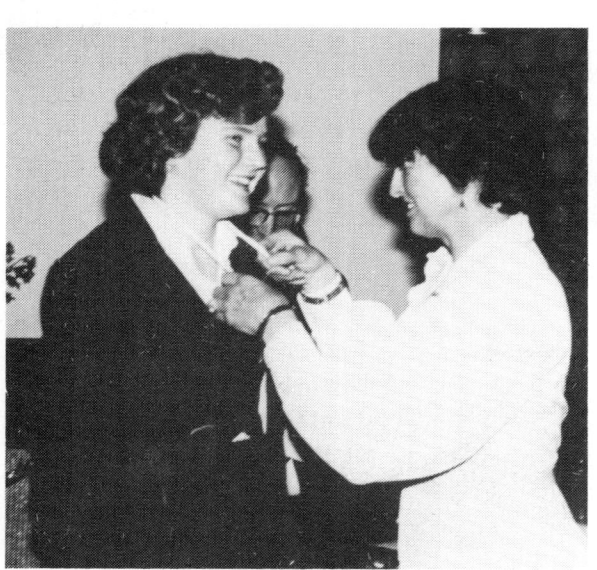

167 (*right*) **The Best Ever**. Bríd Naughton hands over to Fidelma White at the CBS track. They broke the national senior record for 4 x 100 metres along with Nora O'Grady and Noelle Morrissey, 47.8 seconds, at Tullamore, 1980, even though three of the team were still juveniles.

168 (*right*) Peter Gleeson, second from left, and Cyril Whelan, right, tackle two Ballymena stars in an inter-club 800, CBS track, 1981.

169 (*left*) Seán Finn leads out Jim Sheahan (the winner) on his shoulder, – , Robert Denmeade (outside), Clonmel, later Nenagh Olympic Hon Treas, and Jim Moloney (rear, inside), Thurles, in the county senior 1500 championship at the CBS track, 1981.

170 (*right*) Jim Sheahan collects the baton from Peter Gleeson while Robert Denmeade gets Clonmel's in the New Year's Day Round-the-Streets Relay of six legs, each three-quarters of a mile, for Co. Tipperary clubs, 1980.

171 (*left*) **Nenagh Chapter of Junior Chamber** devised an ind(ustrial) ex(hibition) in February 1981 as a showcase for local manufacturing and service industries. (left) Seán Butler, and (centre) Senator David Molony (Fine Gael) meet Jaycee members (l to r): John Gleeson, Paddy Richardson, Mary Walsh (President), Tony Walsh (Project Chairman), and Michael Hannon (PRO).

172 (*right*) Swan Malone, importers of Austrian wine, were co-sponsors of Index '81. In front of their stand, manned by Tomás Malone (right), are members of St. Mary's Secondary School Transition Year mini-company, DELCO: Jennifer Lindsay (Production Manager), – , Monica O'Halloran (Personnel Manager), with Breda Lindsay of Nina Linzi.

173 (*left*) Mary and Noel Shoer visited Ger Clifford at his Nenagh Tool Hire Stand.

174 (*left*) Michael Smith, TD, Minister of State at the Department of Agriculture, was greeted by his Fianna Fáil party colleague, Tony McKenna, MCC, at his B(for Borrisokane) Kenn plastics stand.

175 (*middle, left*) & 176 (*middle, right*) Tommy O'Brien in his fitted kitchen has a visitor, Olive Harris, from the Nenagh Textile stand; his sister Bernadette Treacy, Mrs Mai Treacy, and Brendan Treacy admire some of the fittings. All exhibitors reported increased business; O'Briens got orders for 24 fitted kitchens as a direct result of Index '81.

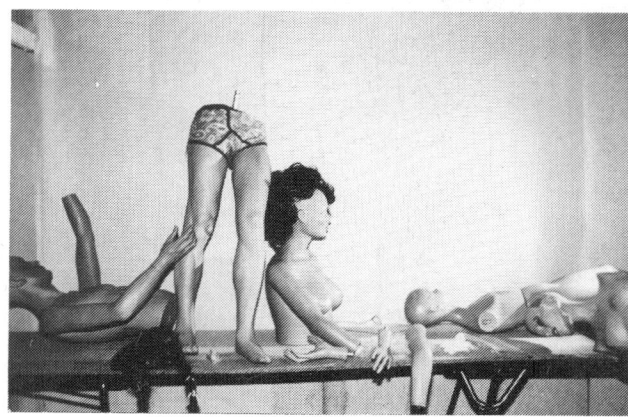

177 (*right*) After the 3,000 visitors to Index '81 had gone …

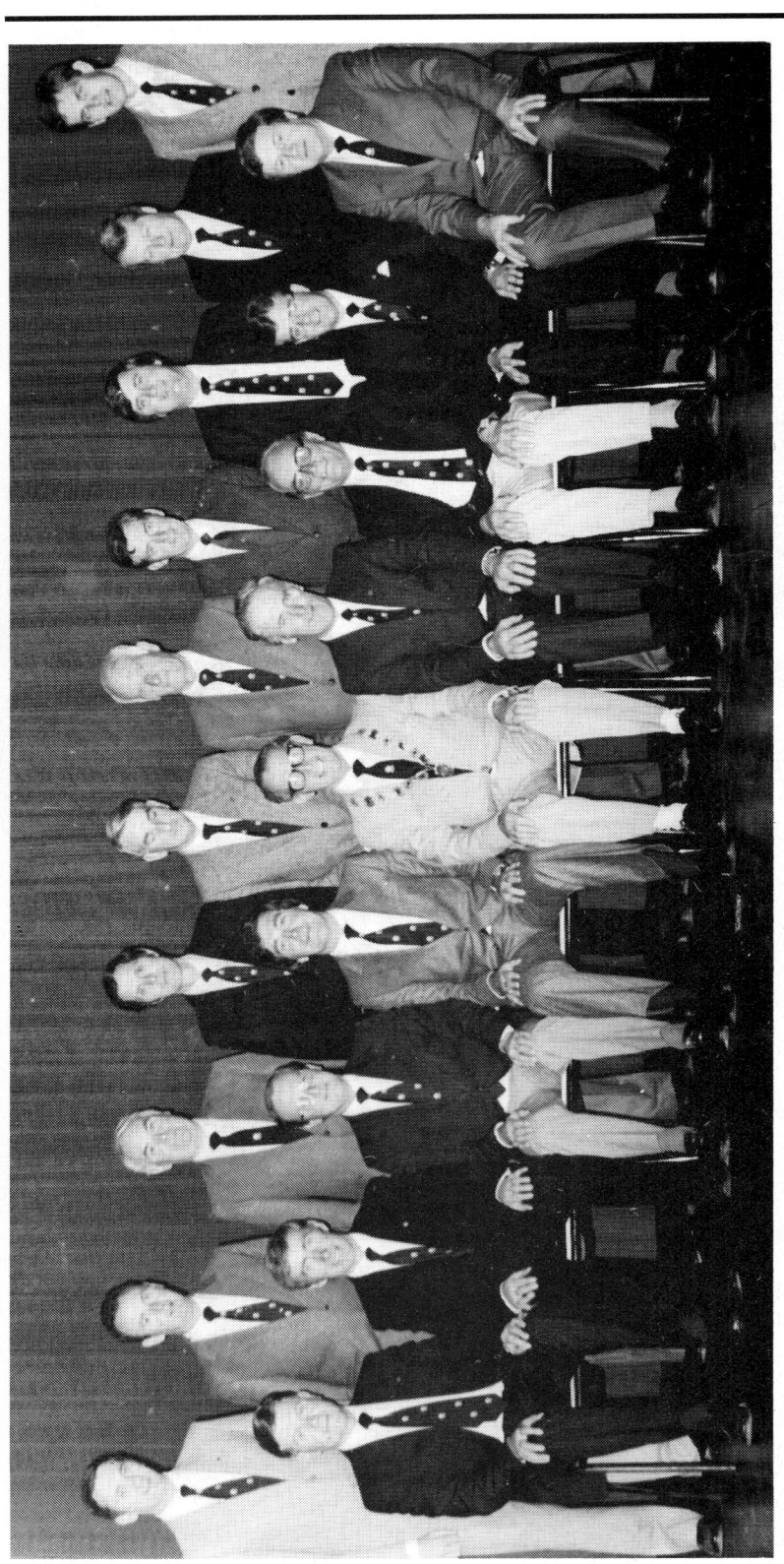

178 Nenagh Lions Club 1984-5. Back (l to r): Gus Carey, Melrose; Ned Hanrahan, Hogan's Pass; John Ryan, Summerhill; Jim McCarthy, Pearse St; Tadgh O'Flynn, Limerick Rd; Peter Smith, Dromin Rd; Brendan Galvin, Brooklands; Tom Harrington, Knockalton Upper; Donal Whelan, Dromin Rd; Frank Maloney, Melrose. **Front:** Billy Talbot, St. Conlan's Rd; Pádraig O'Kennedy, Church Rd; Pat Ryan, Newtown; Noel Cleary, Hon Treasurer, Dromin Rd; Vincent D'Arcy, President, Annbrook; Jim Hughes, Hon Secretary, Carrig; Jim O'Sullivan, Annbrook; Michael Lovett, Dromin; Jim Fallon, St. Conlan's Rd. **Absent from picture:** Henry Cleary, Annbrook; Denis Costelloe, Pearse St. This photo originally appeared in the 1984-5 *Local Telephone Directory* which they updated and republished in 1991 and 1996.

Nenagh Lions Club was founded in 1973, with the primary purpose of identifying, taking on board, and bringing to fruition, projects which would serve to provide a better quality of life for our local community, with special emphasis on the needy, the sick, and senior citizens.

In the area of capital expenditure they provided the equipment in the Coronary Care Unit in Nenagh County Hospital; purchased a site, together with equipment and furnishing, for the Nenagh Day Care Centre; and contributed to the purchase of an ambulance for the Knights of Malta.

179 (*above*) **A Lions Club sponsored walk** stepping it out past the Rialto Cinema, in their first fund-raising venture,1973. **Front** (l to r): Seamus Cleary, Michael Hackett, Joe Gilmartin, Michael Gilmartin, Rodge Coffey (slightly behind), Rev. Eamonn Gilmartin, Michael O'Brien, Noel O'Meara, Dr Richard Fogarty, David and Susan Fogarty. **Behind, to the right:** John Quill, Patrick F. Treacy, John Riggs-Miller, David Hodgins.

180 (*left*) **Johnny McLoughlin, Nenagh Brass Band** coming to the Nenagh Lodge Hotel from tutoring the Nenagh CBS Concert Band in Summerville. He commenced his music on drums with his father in the Ex-Servicemen's Band based in The Hut, Cudville, played trombone with the Legion of Mary Band founded in 1947 [NY 154], and became vice-Chairman of Nenagh Brass Band which was founded in 1979. He was an employee of Irish Aluminium Company/Castle Brand for over forty years. He was a member of the revived St. Patrick's Day Parade Committee, 1979. He died on 16 July 1993. Nenagh Brass Band led the cortege on his removal to St. Mary's of the Rosary church. Members of the CBS band provided a guard of honour that evening and for his funeral.

An Ambulance Unit of the **Order of Malta** was inaugurated in Nenagh in August 1941. The Order has evolved from the Knights of the Order of St John of Jerusalem, founded in the eleventh century. The Order provides first aid teams for all public functions and runs courses for the general public.

The photograph above is a combination of Red Cross members who had completed a home nursing and first aid course, and the first members of the Order of Malta Unit.

181 (*above*) The Red Cross members are **Back** (l to r): Sally Gardiner, St. Patrick's Tce; Dot Brereton, Sarsfield St; Cissie Cleary; – ; Agnes Whelan, Kickham St. **2nd Row:** Mary B. Cleary, Knigh; –; Mai O'Sullivan, Summerhill; – Heaney, Ormond St; –; Pauline O'Sullivan, Kickham St; Louise McConnell, Cudville. **Front:** Mrs Jim O'Sullivan, Kickham St; Bridie Creed, St. Joseph's Hospital; Dr A.D. Courtney, do. (both instructors); –; – Gleeson, Smithfield.

The Order of Malta members (left hand side of picture) (l to r): Corporal John Toohey, Silver St; J. J. McGrath, St. Flannan's St; William J. Heaney, Ormond St; Willie Stronge, Tyone; Seán Hyland, Ormond St; David Herriott, Pearse St. (right hand side): Sgt Willie Irvine, St. Patrick's Tce; Richard Grace, MacDonagh St; Eddie O'Donnell, Ormond St; George Maher, Abbey St; Tom Bennett, a chemist at Herriotts.

182 (*left*) **Nenagh Unit of Malta,** mid-1960s, with the first female members. **Back** (l to r): Tom Keogh, Tyone; Noel Bowler, Hanly's Place; Jimmy Butler, MacDonagh St; Tony Geaney, William St; Ned Carey, Borrisoleigh. **3rd Row:** – ; Pat Whelan, Richmond; Tony Langton, do.; J. Cleary; 'Chubby' Hassett, Tobar Mhuire. **2nd Row:** Richard Grace, Knockanpierce; George Maher, Abbey St; Teresa Gubbins, St. Patrick's Tce; Breda Langton, Richmond; Judy Ryan, Sarsfield St; Nancy Murphy, Tyone. **Front:** Captain O'Gorman-Quin, Regional Director; Willie Stronge, Nenagh; Dr A. D. Courtney, K.M., Nenagh.

183 (*above*) **Nenagh Unit of Malta,** late 1960s. **Back:** (l to r): Rory Flannery, Knockanpierce; Denis Cavanagh, MacDonagh St; Tom Keogh, Tyone; Tony Geaney, William St; Tony Langton, Richmond; Pat Whelan, do.; Michael Moloney, Mitchel St. **Middle:** Cadets Seán Bowler, Hanly Place; Bertie Sherlock, Knockalton Upr; Denis Costelloe, Pearse St; John Keogh, Tyone; Paschal Whelan, Knockanpierce; – ; Paddy Ryan, Summerhill. **Front:** Adjutant George Maher; Lieutenant Willie Stronge, Sgt Richard Grace.

184 (*right*) **The Cadets** 'at ease' in Kickham St after the formalities.

185 (*above*) **Eamonn Coghlan, world champion**, officially opens Ireland's only Indoor Stadium at Ballygraigue, 23 December 1990. He is accompanied by protégés of Tom Holmes 'in the recent drive to re-build the juvenile base', while club and stadium promoters Seán Naughton and Willie Jones applaud: (l to r): Deirdre Hogan, Sinéad Devaney, Jacqueline Kinane, Joanne Mitchell, Michelle O'Gorman, Jennifer Hayden, Clodagh Hayes. He had been termed by the American media, 'Chairman of the Boards' (most American indoor tracks having board surfaces as distinct from Nenagh's more modern tartan).

Devaney has since won national bronze in hurdles and Munster gold, silver, bronze in pentathlon, hurdles and relay, as well as Munster gold and national silver in Schools soccer, and represented Tipperary in Community Games swimming. Hayden has won Munster indoor sprint and relay golds and several county titles. O'Gorman has risen to national individual/team gold, silver, bronze in national BLOE/Community Games 800, cross-country, 6K 'marathon', and javelin.

186 The Back-up. 1 (*opposite, below left*) Breda McKenna (seated), Club Hon Sec, was the controller of programme and results at the national BLOE pentathlon championships at a sunny CBS track, 1978 or 1979.

187 The Back-up. 2 (*opposite, below right*) Patsy Dunne and son from Kilbarron prepare the footwork at a frosty Templemore cross-country venue, while Seán Naughton sorts out the competitors' numbers.

188 (*top, this page*) **Action from the North Final, 1982.** (see page 111) (l to r): Tadgh O'Connor, Roscrea; Philip Kennedy, Éire Óg; – ; Michael Scully, Roscrea; Phil Hennessy, Éire Óg; Jim O'Sullivan, do.

189 (*middle, this page*) Half-time for a break?

190 (*right*) Eamonn O'Toole, Tommy 'Digger' Stanley and Jim 'Rocky' O'Sullivan share after-match craic.

191 (*above, left*) **Women's work is never dull** at Civil Defence pipe drill.

192 (*above, right*) **They also serve who only stand and wait** (l to r): Johnny McGrath, ambulance driver, with Tommy Foley, rescue vehicle driver. Ready for any Emergency …

193 (*below*) **… but where were they when they were really needed?** Not much assistance coming from the crowd either, for the driver of LB 6669 in this evocative scene. Note the more reliable donkey and car tethered in the background.

194 (*above*) **At the Market Cross, early 1950s.** (l to r): Johnny Quinn, Silver St; – ; Donie Morrissey; Eddie Clifford, Dublin Rd; Dessie Ryan, William St; Jack Fogarty, Knigh; Patsy McLoughlin, Silver St; Martin Gleeson, Ballyhogan; James White, William St; – ; John Joe O'Neill, Knockanpierce; Billy Hodgins, do. William J. Heaney had as good an eye for a picture as he had an ear for the makings of a paragraph for his *Guardian* and *Tipperary Star* columns (see his similar study on page 23).

195 (*below, left*) **A Bird in the hand ...**

196 (*below, right*) **Ugh, Babe ...**

Personal Index:

Family and friends appear on the following pages:

_____   _____

_____   _____

_____   _____

_____   _____

_____   _____

_____   _____